MR. TAFT'S SCHOOL

THE FIRST CENTURY

1890 — 1990

by

RICHARD H. LOVELACE

Published by Taft School
First Edition
ISBN 0-9624435-0-6
Printed in the U.S.A.

Dedication

To all of the Taft students, faculty,
parents, and friends, who, during the
school's first 100 years have joined
hands and hearts to make Taft a great
school as it enters its next 100 years.

Foreword

This volume, produced as a part of the school's 100th anniversary celebration, is in some ways an updating and expansion of a predecessor published twenty-five years ago: *Taft: 75 Years in Pictures,* and some of the more memorable contents of the earlier volume have been reproduced. But there is considerably more text, so that the ratio of pictures to prose is approximately 50-50.

Inasmuch as the school has had only four headmasters in its century, it seemed logical and appropriate to organize the history sequentially by headmaster. Very conveniently, Mr. Taft, after considerable prodding from his old boys, produced his own version of the founding of the school in his delightful *Memories and Opinions* (Macmillan 1942). Some forty pages of this invaluable source have been excerpted to serve as the first section of the present history. While Paul Cruikshank's memoirs were never published, they too have been useful in recapturing the twenty-seven years of his tenure. Headmasters Esty and Odden are both highly articulate men and their own "memories and opinions" are near at hand.

Certain sections of school activities — indeed most — obviously overlap and continue from headmaster to headmaster with perhaps only slight variations. Thus, subjects such as athletics, fund raising, and curriculum have been covered as distinct entities in individual chapters.

Geoffrey Elan, an editor of *Yankee Magazine,* once wrote a perceptive column proclaiming the difference between "records" and history. The essay was entitled "How to Write a Dull Town History." Mr. Elan provided three "infallible instructions:" 1. It should be written by a committee. 2. Don't leave anything out. 3. Don't offend anyone. Instead, he advocated the importance of proportion, the avoidance of "reverent reporting of trivia," and summarized the essential duty of the historian "to prune away the inessential facts and avoid what E.B. White called the mistaken notion that everything is important."

Thus, not every outstanding basketball team or dramatic production is represented here. And many people who contributed greatly to the school through the years may not be individually cited. But it is to be hoped that some of the flavor of the rich 100 years of this great school may be sensed in the presentation of the people and events in the pictures and text that follow.

Richard H. Lovelace
South Orleans, Massachusetts

Introduction

In 1965 Dick Lovelace wrote the first major study of the School since Horace Taft's memoirs, *Memories and Opinions.* Dick's seventy-five year history was immediately a great success and today, the School's remaining copies in the visiting room and in the School archives are read with great interest on a daily basis. As we approached our 100th Anniversary, it seemed natural to turn to Dick once again, and so I did to ask him to author our School's Centennial History.

No one could be better prepared to write a history of Taft. Dick Lovelace served on the faculty with distinction and deep loyalty from 1949 until his retirement in 1982. During his years in Watertown, he was a distinguished teacher of English, chaired the department for many years, served as Alumni Secretary and Editor of the Taft School *Bulletin,* and ultimately completed his career as the recipient of the William Sullivan Chair, the highest honor the Taft Board of Trustees can confer upon a member of the English faculty. A gifted teacher, a devoted schoolmaster, and an author blessed with the ability to convey the big picture, Dick has devoted the past three years of his retirement to preparing this wonderful Centennial History. He mixes the reminiscence of alumni and faculty, photographs, and other illustrations with his own insights into the development of our School.

This history tells a wonderful story of how Horace Taft's dreams, ideals, and vision for his School evolved from the modest beginnings of Pelham Manor, New York, into the leading School Taft is today. Each of us in the Taft family, be we student, graduate, teacher, parent or friend, has played a part in the building of this dream. I think you will find your place here even as you enjoy those parts of the story which are new to you. We are indebted to Dick for his labor of love and know that even as he has recorded our story, he has again helped to make ours a better School.

Lance Odden
Headmaster
May 1989

Acknowledgements

Many people have helped produce this volume. The School Archives were, of course, essential, and a great debt is due the late Leslie Manning, School Archivist (and much more) from 1974 to 1985. Anne Romano, the present Librarian, has been consistently helpful in technical areas as well as in suggesting resource material. Many people on the administrative side at the School contributed their skill and knowledge at various times during the last four years. Irene Budzynski typed (beautifully) the entire first draft of the manuscript and Roger Foley then transposed it on his miraculous computers. Jerry Romano, Joan Atwood, Sue Everett, and Julie Reiff in the Alumni Office always responded generously to my queries — often at times when they were hard-pressed with other aspects of their "normal" duties.

Several alumni have been helpful at various stages. Phelps Platt '36 and John Watling '53 both read the manuscript and made thoughtful comments. John Brust '54 and George Fayen '49 provided warm personal recollections of their years as students, and Henry Estabrook's '43 memories of the exciting but disruptive years of World War II have been reproduced in the text.

The Headmaster's secretary, Karyl Scrivener, handled all sorts of administrative details with unfailing courtesy and efficiency. At the very beginning of the project Mr. and Mrs. Charles Allen of Watertown provided vital encouragement and suggestions. Mr. William Scherman of Hanover, N.H., read the entire manuscript and gave generously of his experience in publishing, making invaluable editorial suggestions. Former colleague Samuel I. A. Anderson proofread the manuscript with an exacting eye.

Patsy Odden provided detailed statistical information on the athletic records of Taft teams for the past 100 years and highlighted contemporary athletic achievements. I owe a large personal thank you to John and Carol Noyes for their unfailing hospitality in providing comfortable quarters for me during my monthly trips to Watertown over a period of 3 or 4 years. I am also grateful to Sally Cruikshank, who very graciously made available to me interesting Cruikshank family memorabilia.

Without Headmaster Lance Odden's personal encouragement, astute suggestions about content, and fundamental institutional backing, the project would not have been possible in the first place.

Finally, my wife has borne the highs and lows of the four years of research with patience, providing much-needed encouragement as well as insightful suggestions.

R.H.L.

CONTENTS

1 Horace D. Taft
1890 – 1936

53 Paul Cruikshank
1936 – 1963

97 John C. Esty, Jr.
1963 – 1972

129 Lance Odden
1972 – present

154 Changes in the
Curriculum

164 The Alumni Fund and
Scholarship Aid

168 Capital Funds and
Buildings

177 Athletics

188 Chronology

190 Index

MR. TAFT'S

SCHOOL FOR BOYS

PELHAM MANOR, NEW YORK

MR. HORACE D. TAFT will open a boarding and day school for boys on September 25th, 1890, at Pelham Manor, Westchester Co., N. Y.

The object of the school will be to prepare boys for college.

Pelham Manor is a suburb of New York about fifteen miles from the city. It is situated on Long Island Sound, which is about half a mile from the school, and is accessible by the New York, New Haven and Hartford Railroad (via New Rochelle) and by the Harlem River branch of that road, trains running at all hours. The situation of the school is healthful, quiet and convenient.

The Principal graduated from Yale in 1883 and has been a Tutor in Latin in that University for the last three years.

To be admitted, a boy must be of good moral character and must give evidence of good training in the ordinary English branches. Boarding pupils must be at least thirteen, day scholars at least twelve, years of age. Before being admitted to one of the advanced classes a boy must satisfactorily pass an examination on the subjects studied in the lower classes.

The course will extend over four years and will consist of the studies usually pursued in preparation for the best colleges, careful attention being given to the boy's use of English.

The object of the school is not to prepare boys for college in the shortest possible time. While it is hoped that the influences surrounding the boys will be such as to make them interested and diligent, yet if any are found to fall behind through laziness, after fair warning they will be removed from the school. Those who fail to keep up with the class from lack of ability will be removed to the next class below. Overwork, however, will be guarded against. Promotion and graduation will be for those only who show satisfactory progress. The classes will be small and frequent reports of progress made will be sent to parents.

There will be no lack of recreation for the pupils. Great care will be given to their physical development, daily exercise will be compulsory and a large field will be provided for athletic games. In these the boys will have the companionship of their teachers.

That there may be no divided control, parents are expected to delegate their authority to the teachers during term time. Day scholars are expected to remain until late in the afternoon. Punctuality and regularity will be insisted upon and leave of absence granted for good cause only.

The housekeeping will be in charge of an experienced and competent matron.

The exercises of the day will begin with prayers at 8.45 A. M. On Sundays the boys will attend church in company with a teacher and in the afternoon there will be a Bible lesson and informal talks of a practical character. There are two churches in Pelham Manor, one Presbyterian, the other Episcopal. Each boy will attend the one chosen by his parents.

Each pupil should bring clothes suitable for vigorous physical exercise, over-shoes, rubber boots and rubber coat. All articles of clothing should be marked with the owner's name. The school will furnish bedding, towels and the other articles usually furnished by boarding pupils and to meet this expense a charge of $15 will be made for each pupil on entering, which will cover the whole term of residence.

The charge for boarding pupils will be $600 per annum, for day scholars $200 per annum, one-half payable at the beginning of the school year, the other half on February 1st. Laundry work $0.75 a dozen. Books, stationery, seat in church, at cost. Parents of day scholars who do not wish their sons to depend entirely for their lunch on what they can carry with them can make satisfactory arrangements with the Principal for the supply of what is needed.

The school year will begin September 25th, 1890, and will close June 25th, 1891. The usual holidays will be granted, including a vacation of two weeks at Christmas and one of one week at Easter.

Address until June 25th, 1890,
MR. HORACE D. TAFT,
New Haven, Conn.

After that date,
Pelham Manor,
Westchester Co., N. Y.

Horace Taft

Like all great headmasters, Horace Taft remained always at heart a boy. And because that heart was great and overflowing with understanding and sympathy it responded swiftly to the needs, whether great or small, of the boys of his school. He understood frailties; but he understood as well the potential good; and confident that this good would eventually prevail he set himself to the task of hastening that happy day, and remained to the end of his life an optimist. For myself, and for many of my colleagues in the Headmasters Assocation it was Horace Taft who, more than anyone else, gave color and warmth to the group. Among ourselves we dubbed him Prince of the Headmasters. He will always be just that to me.

—Alfred E. Stearns
Headmaster Emeritus, Andover

HORACE DUTTON TAFT
FOUNDER AND HEADMASTER 1890—1936

Mr. Taft and the Founding of the School

Horace Dutton Taft was born December 28, 1861, in Cincinnati, Ohio. He came from "good Yankee stock on both sides", both his mother's family, the Torreys, and the Tafts having settled first in Massachusetts in mid-17th century. The Taft branch moved to Vermont, where Horace's father, Alphonso, was born. A remarkable man, Alphonso Taft demonstrated his determination to get an education by walking to Yale from his Vermont home. After graduating Phi Beta Kappa in 1833, he taught briefly at Yale, then heeded the siren call of the day to "Go West", and moved to Cincinnati in 1839, where he became a successful lawyer.

He married Fanny Phelps and the children of this marriage were Charles Phelps Taft and Peter Rawson Taft. After Fanny's death, Alphonso Taft married Louisa Torrey. He had become acquainted with her through his Yale classmate, the Reverend Samuel Dutton, whence came Horace Taft's middle name. The couple had five children: Samuel (died in infancy), William Howard, Henry Waters, Horace Dutton, and Fanny Louise.

An outstanding judge in Ohio, Alphonso Taft served in President Grant's cabinet as Secretary of War and Attorney General, and later became Minister to Austria and Russia.

All of the Taft brothers went to Yale, and Horace graduated in 1883. He later recalled that it was at Yale that he formed life-long friendships at that "charming period of life."

An early photo — about 1895 —of the Watertown Post Office. A corner of the Town Hall may be seen on the left. A few years later, the U.S. Government Post Office moved out, and the building became the Post Office Drug Store.

Hockey has been popular from the very first days of the school. The 1906 team scored 41 goals to opponents' 9, losing only to the Yale freshmen.

HocKey TeaM

The 1905 Hockey Team — Undefeated
Perry, Deming, Bingham, Hunt, *Forwards*
J. Lilley, *Cover Point;* Emmons, *Point*
Sellers Allerton, *Goals*

After Yale he studied at the Cincinnati Law School, but disliked the practice of law and, when his friend and Yale classmate Sherman Thacher stopped in Cincinnati en route to Kansas City after graduating with high honors from Yale Law School, he invited Horace to go with him. In 1887 Mr. Taft did go to Kansas City, where he supported himself by tutoring a young boy in arithmetic and algebra. While still there, and dreaming of starting a school, he received a call from Yale to return to New Haven as a Latin tutor.

For three years — 1887 to 1890 — he was a most successful tutor at Yale, but in the fall of 1889, contracted typhoid fever. During his convalescence, he traveled to San Diego, where his parents were staying. While there, he again visited Sherman Thacher, who was starting a school in the Ojai Valley. Mr. Taft returned to Yale more than ever determined to have his own school.

At this point it is appropriate that the rest of the story be told by Mr. Taft himself.

The Founding of the School Excerpted from Horace Taft's *Memories and Opinions*.

At the end of February, 1890, I went back to San Diego for another short visit with my parents, but by the 20th of March, I was in New Haven again and taking my classes. I had not given up the idea at any time of having a school of my own, but was puzzled as to how to go about it. I had sense enough to know that I ought to have some experience in the work I was proposing to take up. I had never been either a pupil or a master in a boarding school. I applied to Mr. William L. Cushing, who had started the Westminster School at Dobbs Ferry, New York, telling him that I should be very glad to teach in his school for a couple of years if he had a position in mathematics, but that I intended to start a school of my own at the end of that time. He and I had become good friends during the first year of my tutorship, when he was also a member of the Yale faculty. He replied that he had a long-legged friend to whom he would be glad to offer a place for *five* years, but he could not consider a shorter term than that. Of course that was very sensible on his part. I was proposing to learn my trade under him and then, when I had made a fair start at it and was worth my salt, to leave and start a school of my own.

Just at that time an opportunity came my way. Mrs. Robert Black of Pelham Manor, New York, was a great friend of my brother Henry, who also lived at Pelham Manor. Her brother had been a roommate of Harry in college, and through him I had come to know Mr. and Mrs. Black very well. Her father had recently died and she was thinking of erecting a school in his memory and proposed that I take the headmastership. I have often wondered whether I should have done better to go farther in finding a subordinate place in some other school, and thus learn the ropes.

The Red House — Pelham Manor. Mr. Taft's School from 1890-1893.

Mrs. Robert C. Black, owner of
the Red House, Pelham Manor,
N. Y.
(Photo courtesy of her grandson, Robert C. Black, III '33)

Certainly I should have learned in a couple of months a great many things that it took me a long time to learn on my own. Yet there were experiences in the Pelham Manor School that were valuable. I accepted the position. The arrangement was tentative on both sides. The school was called "Mr. Taft's School" at the beginning but, as a matter of fact, it belonged to Mrs. Black and I was on a salary, though, of course, the complete management was mine. She owned a residence building which we called the Red House. The last time I visited Pelham Manor it was still stand-ing, but it was no longer red. There was a tiny house next to it which we rented. Some time in the spring, while I was still a tutor at Yale, I had little leaflets printed in which I let the world know what an opportunity was open to it, and sent them around to Yale graduates. I would give a good deal to have one of those leaflets. I should like to see what I promised, but I have never been able to find one.

I was much tickled to get a letter by return mail from a Mr. Eells of Cleveland, written in haste, asking whether I had a room for his boy. It was the first hint I had had that anybody was interested. I replied, calmly, that I had room. I might have added that I could let him have the whole school. Well, replies came slowly during the summer, and in September the list consisted of ten boarding scholars and seven day scholars. At the end of that summer I was in Litchfield, visiting my friend McLaughlin, and I can well remember having more of the feeling of taking a jump in the dark than when I went to Yale as a freshman. I did not know what was coming. The night before I left, I went to call on President Timothy Dwight of Yale, who had a summer home in Litchfield. He was very cordial, sympathetic, and humorous and, at the end, said that I must "be sure to drop in on a sister institution once in a while." I have been dropping in on that sister institution for fifty years.

"Horace, You Have Got To Have A Bed Thirty Feet Wide!"

We had the two houses and we had the promise of the boys, but that was all. Mrs. Black had gone to Europe for the summer. She was to furnish the houses, but she returned from Europe very late and, the night before the school opened, trucks were coming up from New York, bringing the entire furniture for the school — not the kind of trucks we have today, but horse-drawn, and they were traveling all night. The furniture arrived at the same time that the boys and their parents did, and I put both boys and parents to work on the front porch opening boxes. Carpenters were at work upstairs, putting up the beds. It was a most comical beginning of a school. Mr. Black was there, and he was moving around, entertaining parents and boys. He was excellent company and a host in himself. When he had finished, he said to me: "Horace, you have got to have a bed thirty feet wide. Every mother here expects her boy to sleep with you." Indeed, the place was so small that my long arm could almost reach any of them.

Considering how few there were, there was an extraordinary variety among the boys. An undue proportion of them had been in other boarding schools and knew more about the inside of a boarding school than I did. You might have said of them as was said of some emigrants:

True patriots all; for be it understood,
We left our country for our country's good.

You will understand from that how mixed the quality was; and it continued to be true the three years in Pelham Manor, some very good and some very bad. For teachers I had at the beginning a young man, Mr. William Tatlock, who taught all the Greek and some of the Latin, and a young woman, Miss Cowles, who took the small boys. Though there were only seventeen boys, all grades were represented, so that we had a large number of classes of one, three, or five boys. We taught steadily through the school day. I was teaching chiefly Latin and mathematics, though there was hardly anything outside of Greek and modern languages that I did not try my hand at. A headmaster of a small school is expected to do what nobody else will do.

Fourteen of us sat down at the table. That table we still have, and I think it is the only relic of Pelham Manor days.

We were in for a long hard fight. Johnson's line comes to mind:

'Slow rises worth, by poverty depress'd.'

This looks a bit conceited, this assertion that worth was there. I had thought of something very different from this. It was not the lack of physical equipment that troubled me, for, of course, that I could have foreseen. On that side we lacked nearly everything except places to sleep and eat. We had no gymnasium, no ball field, no recitation rooms, or assembly room worthy of the name.

Papyrus Editorial Board — 1897   J. W. Perry; *Editor-in-Chief* Stirling Bell; O. W. White; Standing: F. G. Mason; Lea Hunt

But the little school was more like a tutoring school than one of the regular kind. In the first place, it was impossible to maintain any standard of admission except that of mere good character, because I could not pay the rent and was obliged to take boys in all stages of preparation and do my best for them. All the vitality of the teachers and myself was given to teaching boys who were behind in their work and to the many details which, in a larger, well organized school, could be arranged more easily. It was humiliating to be held in scholarship to the task of preparing for college examinations.

A rare photograph of Mrs. Taft, shown here with husband Horace on the verandah of the Warren House. A gracious and popular presence in the early days of the school, Mrs. Taft died in 1909.

"Discipline was primitive and direct"

Outside the school, life was a little complicated by the fact that there was a girls' school but a short distance from ours. I was troubled by the fact that our arrival doubtless dismayed Mrs. Hazen and her assistants, for we must have been a great nuisance. The girls had had free range over the country, a freedom which the mere presence of a boys' school reduced considerably. My efforts to make ourselves as little objectionable as possible led to rules that were vexatious, and that would have been quite unnecessary but for the close proximity of the other school.

One thing cheered me mightily. I suppose that nothing pleased me so much in my plan for a boys' school as the idea that I might be a lay preacher, that association with boys would give me opportunity for influencing their ideas and ideals. I found close association not only agreeable, but often inspiring, for I began to think that I was achieving some results that had nothing to do with the marking book or college examinations.

Through all my Pelham Manor experience I had the hearty support and friendship of Mr. and Mrs. Black, for which I could not be grateful enough.

The second year at Pelham Manor, we had twenty boarding scholars, and a few more day scholars than we had had the first year. We rented two other residence buildings, quite as unfit for school purposes as the first two, and they were at some distance. We had nothing fit for a school, I think, except ambition. We certainly had a very low standard in scholarship; but we were aware of it, and we struggled hard. The teaching was poor. You cannot teach all day, and teach all kinds of subjects, and teach well. I think that I may claim that the boys profited a good deal by original work in geometry, in which I was pretty strong. Discipline was very primitive and direct. I had a room in the middle of the Red House on the second floor, and I could reach almost any boy. I waked the boys up in the morning, pulling the blankets off when necessary. There ought to have been a Mark Twain there to describe that school.

In my stay in Pelham Manor I learned a good deal about a headmaster's work, even if a large part of it consisted of learning how not to do it. Moreover, I am inclined to think that I had far more than my share of boys who needed peculiar handling; and, from the memories of those days reported by the old boys, I think that I was not as unsuccessful as might have been expected from the hit-or-miss methods which I have described. In any case, I enjoyed living in such intimate association with the boys, and the experience I had in the small school was of great value to me when the school became larger.

The School Moves To Watertown

Before the end of the first year at Pelham I came to two important decisions. One was that I would marry a certain lady in New Haven, if she consented. She did consent. She was Miss Winifred Thompson of Niagara Falls, New York, and at the time was teaching in the New Haven High School. I had become acquainted with her through my sister when the latter came on to see me through the attack of typhoid fever. We became engaged the spring of my first year in Pelham Manor, and were married at the end of the second year.

The other important decision was that Pelham Manor was no place for the kind of school I hoped to build. We had no building and no chance for a building. The reputation of the climate of the place at that time was not too good and we were altogether too near New York. The consequence was that during the third year at Pelham Manor my wife and I were busy making trips to various places in search of a situation for a school. I had no money and, therefore, it was necessary to find a ready-made building of some sort. We thought of three places in Litchfield, Connecticut, and made numerous trips there. Everybody was most cordial, and many times since then Litchfield people have told me how much they wished I had come to Litchfield, that I should have received a very warm welcome. I always replied that I thought so, but that I needed a great deal more than a warm welcome. As McLaughlin [a friend of Mr. Taft's from Litchfield] had been so dear a

1896 Football
John B. Lear, *Captain;* Dean Welch, *Manager.*
J. Lear, *Left Half Back;* Townshend, *Full Back;* G. Lear, *Right Half Back.*
Gutherie, *Left Guard;* O. White, *Quarter Back;* Welch, *Right Guard.*
L. White, *Left Tackle;* Merriman, *Center;* Bell, *Right Tackle.*
Barnett, *Left End;* McIlhenny, *Sub End;* Lloyd, *Right End.*

The first year in Watertown. The entire school, faculty and students, is pictured here on the steps of the Warren House. Mr. Taft is in the center of the back row.

friend of mine, I had always felt a special interest in Litchfield and I was glad to be able to settle finally within eleven miles of the town. This search, coupled with the business of running a school, made the year a very active and restless one.

Kingsbury Curtis, who was in the class after me in college, met my brother Henry in New York and said: "I hear Horace is looking for a place for a school. I am interested in just the right place for him."

When this was passed on to me I asked, "Where in the world is Watertown, Connecticut?" and was told that it was somewhere near Waterbury.

11

The Warren House

All of my old boys remember Mrs. Buckingham and her two sons. The Buckinghams and the Curtises owned the old hotel, the Warren House. I got into touch with Mrs. Buckingham's brother, Thomas McLean, and Mrs. Taft and I went up to Watertown in February of 1893 to look the hotel over.

I remember the visit well — both the pleasure of meeting the Buckingham family, who were very cordial and helpful and have been intimate friends ever since, and the chill of the visit to the hotel. It was a forsaken place. The building had been closed all winter and was cold and dirty. Nevertheless, it seemed to offer a better opportunity than anything we had seen. The total area was six acres. The building had been erected in 1866. The Wheeler & Wilson Sewing Machine Company had started in Watertown and was so profitable that a number of the biggest investors were wondering how to invest their money. Fortunately for me, some of them undertook the building of this hotel. It flourished for many years and had quite a reputation, though I had never heard of it. It had, however, come on evil days, the fine modern hotels on the shore and in the mountains proving to have much greater attraction.

I leased the house for five years, with the privilege of purchase, and gave my note to Mrs. Black for all that she had spent on the school in Pelham Manor. Thus I paid my debt to her financially, though there was a debt of gratitude which could never be repaid. I succeeded in borrowing ten thousand dollars and went to work making the house fit for our purpose. I wish I could remember all the changes we made in that old building in forty years. We put in new plumbing and heating and erected a

The Warren House.
"We lived to think of that old building as a dreadful handicap, but I remember that, after Pelham Manor, it seemed like Paradise. In every respect it was a big step forward."

H. D. T. — Memories and Opinions

An important school building from 1893 to 1928, it first housed the entire school, but after the construction of the Annex (1908) and the Main Building (now Horace D. Taft Building) in 1912, it served as the school infirmary until it was torn down in 1928 to make way for the construction of the Charles Phelps Taft Building.

wooden building for a gymnasium. In the summer of '93 my wife and I moved what furniture we had from Pelham Manor, took a room in the big building, and wrestled with carpenters and plumbers, meantime receiving the parents who were interested in enrolling their boys.

Getting ready for the opening date was a desperate struggle, and many were the prophecies that we could not do it. But we succeeded with the exception of one thing. The floors in all the corridors were extremely noisy, and the matting which had been ordered at Sloane's did not arrive. After many telegrams we found that Sloane's had sent the matting to Watertown, New York — the first of many mistakes of that kind. We lived to think of that old building as a dreadful handicap, but I remember that, after Pelham Manor, it seemed like Paradise. In every respect it was a big step forward. Everything, however, had to be used for something it had never been meant for and, occasionally, comical things happened.

"Three Beers and Some Pretzels to Room 32"

We tore down the partitions of rooms around the hotel office and made the whole space into a school and assembly room. The ceiling was low, but the floor space would answer. The master sat on the platform where the hotel clerk had been. We had disconnected the wires from the different rooms to the clerk's desk, so that a boy could not ring at his pleasure, but there was a speaking tube from each floor to the clerk's desk, intended for the use of the hotel servants. A young master was holding study hour and endeavoring, as usual, to keep it quiet, when a voice boomed down through that speaking tube: "Three beers and some pretzels to Room 32, and be quick about it." That study hour was ruined. However, a little plaster corrected the trouble.

Another of the group owning the Wheeler & Wilson Sewing Machine Company, having plenty of money, had built a race track in the field opposite the present golf house and had bought fast horses. A quicker way to get rid of money could not be devised. The race track had long since been given up, and I rented the space inside of it for a ball field. The draining system had broken down, so that in wet weather it was swampy. At the beginning of the first year the weather was very dry and there was nothing to indicate the true character of that field. The boys rushed up to the field and laid out a football gridiron in the part of the great space available which was nearest level. When the heavy fall rains came, we were playing football in a regular swamp. I remember the opening game. In the very first run which was made, the whole crowd went down with a splash, and from the bottom of the pile came a voice: "Help! Help! I'm drowning." We afterward moved to the highest part of the field. It was rougher and more sloping, but not so wet, though the time never came when it was a comfortable place to play in.

We piped water from a spring near the ball field to a big tank at the top of the school, and thus got along fairly well in that respect. Our drinking water came from a well that was just outside the old kitchen. It had been advertised by the hotel as clear, sparkling water. We bragged about it a good deal. We drank it. However, the modern scientific idea of sanitation was taking hold and after some years, just for form's sake, I had the water of that well analyzed. Except that of bubonic plague, I do not think there were any germs missing. We filled up the well with ashes and dirt, and that was the end of the clear, sparkling water.

One difficulty with the old hotel was the marked difference in the size and desirability of the rooms. That is what is wanted in a hotel. Higher charges are made for the more desirable rooms. Of course this cannot be done in a school. One room would be palatial in size and, perhaps, be a corner room, but we always refused to put more than two boys into a room. The next room would be half the size. The assignment of rooms sometimes left a little hard feeling because of the tremendous difference between them.

Light From Manufactured Gas

We had neither city gas nor electricity. There was a machine in a little house back of the main building which manufactured gas from gasoline. Except in the schoolroom we depended upon that gas entirely for light. At the beginning the flame was very rich and smoky, so that all the ceilings were "smoked up." The light then ran down and became very thin, until we moved something up a notch, when the richness and the smoke began again, and so on. We depended upon lamps in the big schoolroom. The gymnasium took fire the first year, but was saved by the fire department. When I inquired I found that two boys had been looking at a number of barrels of gasoline which had been brought up to fill the gas machine. The barrels stood just back of the wooden gymnasium, and had on them a kind of frosting. One of the boys bet the other that that frosting would burn. He won. Those barrels made a glorious flame and almost finished us.

Nobody could ever have given a warmer welcome to electric light than we did when our connection with the Watertown powerhouse was established.

To finish the tale of our physical handicaps, the old building was entirely of wood and, once on fire, would have burned like tinder. "Firetrap" was the word most commonly used, and many parents, coming to consider placing their boys there, took one look at the building and departed. Those who left their boys with us commented so often on the fire hazard that it got on my nerves. Of course we had a night watchman and every precaution was taken, but the fear would not down. I remember that when, twenty years later, we had the new building and used the second floor of the old building as an infirmary, my dear sister-in-law, Mrs. Charles Taft, smiled and said: "That's the proper idea. If we burn anybody, it ought to be the unfit."

Each floor of the Warren House had one bathroom, serving all the boys and masters living there, and on one floor there was an extra one for a master's wife. This was hard on the masters, but a boy suffers no privation so philosophically as a restriction of his bathing facilities. Some primitive shower baths in the gymnasium served the athletes.

The Beginning of School Loyalty and Good Traditions

With all these handicaps, we still felt that we had made a long step upward. We began, in 1893, with five masters besides myself. There were thirty boarding scholars and a number of day scholars from Watertown and Waterbury. The Waterbury boys had to come by train, which fact cramped us a bit in making our schedule, as we had to make our hours fit the hours of the train service. The institution took on something of the aspect of a real school. The scholastic work was divided more or less definitely into departments. The boys were divided into five classes, from top to bottom. The younger classes were larger in proportion to the older ones than they had been. The standard of scholarship was slowly rising (it could hardly have fallen) and discipline was firmer, but not less human. On the whole, I had learned a good deal about the job. Moreover, the masters took hold with a will, school loyalty became strong, and good traditions began to supplant bad ones. I was striving hard, and with success, to implant in the older boys' minds a feeling of responsibility to the school, and the monitorial system which I had begun took shape and acquired strength. For all that, it was only by contrast with Pelham Manor days that one could have called it a good school.

Many things gave me confidence, however. The mere fact that we had improved so much was one. Another was my growing pleasure in contact with the boys in groups and separately, and my feeling of confidence in the loyalty and friendship of both boys and masters.

Among the masters, I must mention Olin Coit Joline, whom the great majority of the old boys remember with affection. He served the school faithfully for thirty-two years as a teacher of Greek, but his most important contribution was made in those early years. He was a born disciplinarian, kindly but firm, and had had boarding-school experience, which most of us lacked and which made him a tower of strength in the government of the little institution. He was the only one of the masters who began with the school in Watertown to serve beyond the first two or three years, the only one to see the growth and improvement of which we dreamed. The close bond between him and the boys of those early days remained strong to the day of his death.

One of the five masters was Frederick Winsor, who was afterward the Headmaster of the Middlesex School, in Concord, Massachusetts. I feel that there is a peculiar bond between the old boys who were with us in those early days, say the first ten years, and myself. Our association was very close. As I look back I can see that I was learning my trade at their expense, though they never seemed to hold that against me.

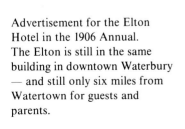

Advertisement for the Elton Hotel in the 1906 Annual. The Elton is still in the same building in downtown Waterbury — and still only six miles from Watertown for guests and parents.

15

Watertown — A Friendly Community

We had settled in a friendly community. Apparently most of the neighbors were glad to have the old hotel building occupied by a school. Many of them placed their boys with us as day scholars, and the reception accorded to the school and to me personally was cordial in the extreme. The warmth of this friendship, which still continues, has been a source of immense pleasure and inspiration to me, and has added to the pleasures in life of the entire school, masters and boys. The Buckinghams, the Heminways, and the Merrimans were most prominent in the life of the town and helped in every way possible; but there were many others, both in Watertown and in Waterbury. Mrs. John Buckingham, whom hundreds of old boys well remember with affection and gratitude, was outstanding in her friendship and loyalty.

Involvement In Village Life

Both masters and boys took part in village life to an extent that was later impossible. They were prominent in amateur theatricals, and their assistance was welcomed by the neighbors. In the first year a firebug caused intense excitement in town for a week, a blaze of some sort being started every night. We were especially alarmed because of the inflammable material of the school itself, and the proximity of the big stable which was part of the hotel property, and which, with its large quantity of hay, would have gone up in flames in a twinkling. If that had happened it would have been almost impossible to save the school. We had extra watchmen around at night, and the boys found a pleasurable excitement in the whole thing. It ended in a great conflagration which destroyed Citizens' Hall, a large building used for theatricals and public meetings. The boys proved themselves splendid firemen and earned the admiration of all who saw the fight by saving a building next to the hall when others had given it up. The arrest of a young fellow on suspicion put a stop to the danger and the excitement.

The boys took in the town meetings, which still had a flavor of old New England, and had some of the ancient characters whose individuality made such meetings interesting. Though the boys could not vote, they felt a live interest in the proceedings, and their sense of humor was frequently stirred.

We attended the Episcopal church in a body and sat in the seats assigned to us in a front corner of the church. I suspect that we did not add to the feeling of reverence which befits such services, though we swelled the size of the congregation. Herbert N. Cunningham was the clergyman and the faithful chaplain of the school. Two of his boys have become popular and influential clergymen, Raymond in Hartford, and Gerald in Stamford. That compulsory church service was a trial, because the services could not be fitted to the needs and development of the boys. Some of the boys were strong dissenters, in the English sense of the word, and one boy asked me, "Mr. Taft, don't you think it would be better to have extemporaneous prayers instead of the cut-and-dried sort we have in church?"

"My boy," I said, "I always prefer an extemporaneous prayer until I hear one. Then I prefer the beautiful language of the prayer book."

Sunday Suppers

In those early years I began having, at Sunday supper in my own apartment, as many boys as my table would hold — a custom which now, after fifty years, I am still carrying on, though retired. Of course, there were many informal gatherings, and I think nothing helped more in the promotion of the right spirit than the casual gathering in a boy's room of a group, the discussion covering any subject from European politics to the last unpopular rule adopted by the faculty. In the main, what a boy needs is to understand the point of view of the masters. He is generally willing to agree that the objective aimed at is right. When he is asked for another method of reaching it, and can suggest none, he begins to feel that his criticism is unfounded.

Most schools send home regular reports of the progress of the boys. I made a regular practice of this and put the report in the form of a letter covering not only the boy's scholastic standing, but his industry and general conduct. These reports I regarded as very important, not only because they kept me in touch with the parents and kept them in touch with the development of the boys, but because they made necessary for me interviews with the masters and a review of the progress and development of each boy. It is easy to say that I could have held this review without writing letters, but it is a desirable thing to have a time table which makes certain performances necessary. I tried hard to tell the exact truth, and I soon acquired the reputation of writing very pessimistic letters. I still think that the reports were fair and am not at all shaken in that opinion by the fact that they differed in many cases from the estimates of the boys and their parents. I was aware that a good many schoolmasters gave rose-colored views of the progress of boys in order to please the parents. It is possible that I leaned over backward in my determination to be honest.

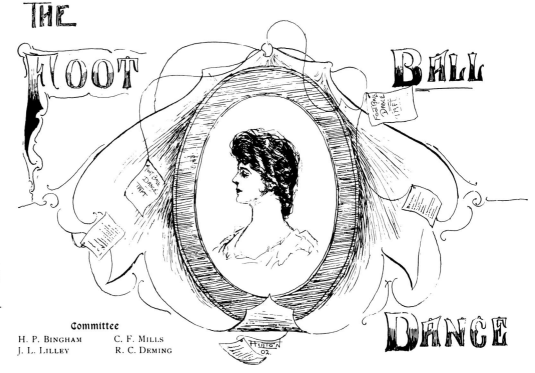

For many years the most important social occasion at the school was the Football Dance, held at the end of the season. This handsome illustration (shades of Charles Dana Gibson) is from the 1906 Annual.

Committee

H. P. BINGHAM   C. F. MILLS
J. L. LILLEY   R. C. DEMING

17

Cast
Mr. Golightly, Henry Hull
Captain Phobbs, Beverly Stapler
Captain Spruce, Corlies Adams
Morland, E. Niles Welch
Sam, Julian Bishop
Mrs. Major Phobbs, Phelps Platt
Mrs. Captain Phobbs, Edward Stevens
A. Waiter, Charles Waller
Ladies, Harden Pratt
Carl Hanna

Committee
Henry Hull, *Chairman;*
Beverly Stapler; *E. Niles Welch*

1907 — "Lend Me Five Shillings"
presented by The Taft Dramatic Club

A dear friend of mine from Savannah, a lady who had a boy in the school, reported to me an amusing conversation with another Savannah mother who had two boys with us. These boys had been in a Virginia school from which glowing reports went home at stated intervals. The mother at some gathering said humorously that she had thought from the Virginia reports that she had two budding geniuses, but that now she was coming to feel that her two boys were mentally lacking. She said that she was inclined to withdraw the boys, but that her husband had risen in his wrath and said, "Thank God, I have found an honest schoolmaster," and had vowed that the boys should not set foot in Georgia again till he had better reports. The lady added, "And now I never expect to see my boys again."

Much later, when the old hotel building was torn down to make way for the big extension, I had forgotten that copies of my old reports were stored in the attic. As wreckers went to work with a vengeance, those copies were scattered far and wide. The boys picked them up and were interested to find that my style and severity were still what they had always been. One boy was immensely pleased to find a copy of a letter which I had written to his grandfather about his father when the latter was a pupil in the school. It was a pretty savage letter, and the father complained to me that it cramped his style a good deal in dealing with his boy.

There is not much to tell over a long period of years, except the slow but steady growth of the school and its gradual improvement. We had a Phi Beta Kappa student at Yale about the turn of the century, the first in a long line of them, and some boys who took the first places in their college classes, these honors marking a rising standard of scholarship in the school and an improvement of standards in literature, spirit, discipline, and life in general.

The new ideas in education had not affected boarding schools at that time, and we followed the old-fashioned curriculum. The great majority of our boys went to Yale, most of them taking the academic course. The examinations were practically the same for all the boys, the only choice, as I remember it, being between French and German.

Many activities flourished outside of college preparatory work, and we were gradually growing nearer to the attainment of our ambition to educate the whole boy. Athletics, of course, flourished immediately. A school paper promptly started, also a glee club and a band. As to the quality of the music, the less said the better. Many years after, an old boy presiding at a reunion congratulated the school on the splendid development of our glee club. He said, "In our day, when the glee club burst into song, the cry was, 'Women and children first.'"

The year 1909, which began so gloriously for us, with the Inauguration [of President Taft] and jollification, ended very sadly. My wife fell ill in the fall and died in December. It is the kind of blow that divides a man's life in two. But in the memory of that winter I have also the memory of the way the masters and their wives and the boys rallied round.

There was nothing to do but to throw myself into the work of the school as completely as possible. Fortunately that was easy to do. Things were driving. The school was growing. We built an addition which we called the Annex; but we still needed room and, moreover, had a growing sense of the tremendous handicap we had in our physical equipment.

We planned to build a new school on the top of Nova Scotia Hill, which our old boys will remember as being northeast of the town and giving a splendid outlook over the valley stretching toward Waterbury. I bought three farms, which would have given us about three hundred acres. It became evident, however, that the expense involved in erecting new buildings and abandoning all of the old plant would be beyond our means. Some years later I succeeded in selling the farms with a slight loss.

Harley Roberts

One might think from what I have said
about the school that it was built by my
own efforts. Nothing could be farther
from the truth. Of the masters, their
loyalty and efficiency, and their share in
the work I hope to speak later; but at
this point I must write about Harley F.
Roberts. Nobody can know as well as
myself how much the school owes him.
He had graduated at the Western
Reserve University, had taken a
graduate course at Yale in Latin, and
had been a tutor in Yale for two or three
years. In 1897 I invited him to be the
head of the Latin department of the
school, and he accepted. He was a man
of amazing energy, and his single-
minded devotion to whatever cause
enlisted his sympathy was extraordinary. He was a tremendous driver,
and never could understand the failure
of boys or men to come up to his own
standard. He was up at six in the
morning, prepared to help any boys who
needed it, working with his classes and
with individuals till late at night, taking

time only for exercise, and in this
exercise using up enough energy for two
men. His whole soul was wrapped up in
the school. He had a certain lack of tact
and a strange inability to know what
other people were thinking about him,
and was at times tremendously surprised
to find the very hostile attitude of
certain classes or individuals toward him
when his strenuous pressure was entirely
unappreciated. This came partly from a
lack of a sense of humor. But many,
even of those who disliked him, afterward
came to appreciate how much they owed
him for his training in the elements of a
difficult language, training that bore
fruit in college. Many were broad-minded
enough, even when under the harrow, to
see how wholeheartedly he gave himself
to others and to the school.

Many were the tales of his memory,
his concentration, and his ability to
carry on two or three activities at the
same time. I remember going into his
room early one morning and finding a
boy sitting at his desk and apparently
translating Caesar to a blank wall. I
heard a splashing of water through the
curtain and a voice saying, "Give that
sentence again — that's not a genitive."

He knew the texts by heart and
consequently his whole attention and
vitality were given to the class. It was
impossible to sleep in his recitation.

He grew in influence and power in the
school, and in 1909 was made second in
command. A goodly part of the
improvement of the school, especially
the improvement in the standard of
scholarship, was due to him.

Incorporating the School

In 1912 we incorporated the school. It had been my private property up to that time. I took five-sixths of the stock, and Mr. Roberts one-sixth. I put in all the school property, all the debts having been paid; and he put in money enough, according to our calculation, for the remaining sixth. We issued bonds and raised $300,000 and planned to build the same building we had planned for the Hill. We bought land enough to give us many times the elbowroom we had had before. William E. Curtis, who was our neighbor on the east and north and had always been a loyal friend of the school, sold us thirteen acres on the most generous terms. Thanks to many good friends, and especially to my brother Charlie and his wife, we sold the bonds and raised the $300,000. The new building and the land, however, cost a good deal more than that. We had room for a ball field, additional tennis courts, and a large space for sewage disposal, an expensive proposition.

We moved in, in sections. I was the last to come over from the old building, and I was established in my new quarters in February of 1914. I was no businessman or bookkeeper, but I could tell by rule of thumb how much money we could make with a certain number of boys, and I counted on our paying the debt fairly promptly. I reckoned without the Kaiser. As I have said, we were established in the new building at the beginning of 1914. That summer the war began. Prices went sky-high, and it took a good deal longer to pay that debt than we expected.

A much-used area located under the "old" dining room. In the early days — as shown above — it was the school auditorium and stage. Later it was a Biology Laboratory, and is now used as a maintenance shop and storage area.

Founding Black Rock State Park

For a long time Harley had been troubled in regard to the beautiful region between Watertown and Thomaston, feeling that the whole section ought to belong to the public. I remember lying on the sofa in his room one evening while he walked up and down, emphasizing his views on this matter. He had been through the woods that day. I said: "I quite agree with you. Why don't you do it, yourself?"

"I will. How much will you give?"

I laughed, thought a bit and said, "A thousand dollars."

"Good! I'll match that!" And then he started. He raised forty-seven thousand dollars, with which he bought great tracts of land and received besides much woodland gratis belonging to the factories of Waterbury. The result of his efforts was that a very extensive and beautiful tract of land has been turned over to the state, the larger part of it under the jurisdiction of the State Forest Commission, a small part of it in the center being put under the jurisdiction of the State Park Commission. This was a tremendous public benefaction. No other man could have done it, and he could not have done it five years later. Too many purchases were being made by private parties. It is a great monument to a very public-spirited citizen.

I am greatly pleased that the school reception room has been named "The Roberts Room," and that the inscription and his picture recall the man. Perhaps some day a more substantial memorial may be contrived for one who was a very true and self-sacrificing worker for the school.

The War's Effect on the School

Of course the excitement caused by our own entry into the war, and the interest in it, were intense. The boys could not be held. We must have drill and a West Point graduate. I laughed and told them that West Point graduates were not to be had. Then they must have a Regular Army officer. Said I, "Boys, the United States Government is not going to be greatly excited when it hears that the Taft School is going to drill." A master in the school had been at Plattsburg [a United States Army Training Camp], and he undertook the drilling. This was a great disappointment to the boys, for it seemed like an extension of classwork. However, they were eager and went at it, and kept up in fine spirit till the Armistice. Unfortunately, we did not get our uniforms till just before the Armistice, and we kept up the drills till the spring vacation. We had to justify those uniforms. The drill became a dreadful bore when there was no prospect of Army service, and the change back to regular athletics was a tremendous relief.

The boys had an idea that the standard of the school was decidedly too high and the work too severe, in which I did not agree with them. When the Germans were attacking Verdun and Marshal Petain issued his thrilling slogan "Ils ne passeront pas" the boys remarked that the French had nothing on the Taft School, for the motto of the masters had always been "They shall not pass."

I will not stop to say much about the Armistice. Of course it was the biggest event of the kind in our national history, except the ending of the Civil War. My incredulity and caution prevented us from celebrating the fake Armistice a few days before the real one, but when the time came and the bells rang and the whistles blew, about four o'clock in the morning, I said to Harley, "There is nothing to do but celebrate the boys right off their legs." And that we did. We had a big bonfire, returned to the school by six o'clock in the morning for breakfast, marched and paraded till there was nothing left of us. Harley, not knowing, of course, what was coming, had provided for a patriotic speech by some orator in the old auditorium under the dining room. Those patriotic boys came down, but they were so tired and sleepy they could hardly hold their heads up. Whether the orator felt repaid, I do not know. However, the next morning at my table a boy said, "I don't suppose I shall ever have as much fun again in one day as I did yesterday." I think that represented fairly the feelings of the school.

I "reminisced" before the student body a few years ago and told about the Armistice. I was taken to task by one of the ladies, who said that I did not tell all of the story. She said that in the great excitement of that early morning, when the neighbors came in at half-past five, I kissed all the ladies and girls. The voice of slander is never silent. In any case, the occasion deserved it. I would do it again — that is, provided I did do it. At six o'clock all the neighbors went in with me to the school breakfast, and all was hilarity. When the breakfast had started I rapped for silence and said that in the midst of our pleasure we ought not to shirk our duty, that there would be a special study period from eight to ten. The boys looked blank till I added, "Tomorrow morning." There was enthusiastic applause, which was increased when I added that all demerits would be canceled. It happened that the list of demerits was an especially long one at that time, so that a number of boys felt that the war had not been fought in vain.

That winter occurred the dreadful epidemic of influenza, and we went through the same struggle that came to all of the schools and colleges. The infirmary quickly overflowed, and two corridors in the main building were set aside for the sick. The school looked like a battlefield. Of course we got all the nurses we could, competing in this with other schools, colleges, and private families, and then took "trained assistants" until Miss Lowry, our head nurse and guardian angel, said: "For heaven's sake, don't get me any more trained assistants. They don't even know how to take a temperature." One mother, who had been a trained nurse, came up from New York, donned her old nurse's uniform, and took charge of a corridor. Others helped as they could. I shall never forget the courage of Mrs. E. Hershey Sneath from New Haven. Her boy was the only one who died. She saw that everything possible was being done for her boy and then reported to Miss Lowry, saying, "I am not a nurse, but I am a good strong woman and I can carry trays, clean the rooms, or do anything else that will help." Bravely she faced the inevitable.

"The Grove." Most of these lovely old elms are now gone.

The School Expands Again

Time went on and the school still grew in numbers. A few years after the Armistice, the generosity of Mrs. William Rockefeller provided us with our new athletic field. Meantime, we had been paying off the debt. That task was finished about 1926. What next? The old hotel was still an important part of our equipment. It was still an unfit place for the infirmary, the servants' quarters, and the laboratories; it was as much of a firetrap as ever. We did not wish to increase the number of pupils and, consequently, we could not look for increased revenue. Moreover, Roberts and I owned all the stock of the school and, in case of the death of one of us, the ownership and management would be a complicated affair. These troubles we could avoid by turning the school over to a Board of Trustees and making it a non-profit institution. In that case, if I died, the trustees would choose the new headmaster and carry on. Besides, in that case we could go out and ask for funds for the school as properly as the president of Yale, whereas we could ask for no contributions for a privately owned school. So that is what we did.

The First Board of Trustees

In 1927 we turned the school over to fifteen trustees, all named in the original charter. One class consisted of five old boys who were to be replaced by election by the alumni. The first class of trustees, however, has elected several old boys, so that the majority of the number consists of boys who have been through the school.

The drive for two million dollars which we decided upon was interesting but strenuous. We profited by the experience of Hotchkiss and other schools and put the drive into the hands of the experts. Before these experts got through, it seemed to me that they knew a good deal more about the school than I did. A good part of their work, however, consisted in organizing committees of old boys in different parts of the country, which involved much labor on my part as I was the only one who knew all the graduates. It involved, also, strenuous speaking trips, which meant, of course, reunions with old boys and their parents, that were very enjoyable but quite exhausting.

The old study hall, located above the dining room. In the late 1960s it was transformed into a fine airy Art Room, where Art Instructor Mark Potter '48 has held sway ever since.

A Drive for Two Million Dollars

The Annex under construction. Started in 1908, the structure was completed in 1910, and served first as "The Lower School", occupied by six married masters and 65 new boys. At some indeterminate time, it ceased to house just "new boys"; instead it served as dormitory quarters usually for Upper Middlers and numerous faculty until it was demolished in October 1963.

The Annex in its prime.

By far the largest gift of the campaign came from Edward Harkness: five hundred thousand dollars as an endowment fund. I have already spoken of my brother and sister-in-law, Mr. and Mrs. Charles P. Taft, who always helped in every way and contributed three hundred thousand dollars in this drive. Henry P. Bingham contributed one hundred thousand and his sister, Mrs. Dudley Blossom of Cleveland, seventy-five thousand. We raised the two millions, at least on paper. The trouble was that the campaign was run in the usual way and subscriptions were asked on a five-year basis. If we had pushed for immediate payment or for payment in three installments, we probably could have collected almost all of it. Payments were prompt and were willingly made till the depression struck us, when two hundred thousand remained unpaid. We had counted on spending more than the two millions and had gone ahead with our building program on the basis of the subscriptions. The expense beyond the two millions, added to the two hundred thousand not paid, made a much more substantial debt than we expected, and the depression did not help us in paying it.

I found considerable trouble in adequately thanking Ed Harkness for his generous gift. Of course I wrote him at once. I tried to see him personally, but each time that I was in New York he was out of town. At last I found him in his office and said, "Mr. Harkness, you are a hard man to catch, but I have made it a rule in my life whenever a man gives me half a million dollars to thank him in person."

One of the first buildings constructed during the great building boom of 1910-13 was a new gymnasium, adjacent to the Warren House. Until 1956 it was known as the "New Gym"; at that time it was replaced by a new gym (and the Black Squash Courts) and then became the "old Gym" until 1985, when both structures were entirely gutted to emerge, phoenix-like, as the new Arts and Humanities Wing.

As soon as we felt sure of the success of the drive, we went at the task of building. James Gamble Rogers was our architect, and association with him was a very agreeable part of the proceeding. We began with the new infirmary and the servants' house, as it was necessary to tear down the old white building. When these were completed we built the second part of the new school.

I have not meant to give the impression that the growth of the school consisted only in increasing in numbers. It is fair to say that the school made a steady improvement from the beginning except, perhaps, during the war years. The older boys' feeling of responsibility for the school varied from year to year but, on the whole, grew stronger. The standard of scholarship rose. We could see it in the school itself, and could see it reflected in the records in the College Board examinations and in the college careers of the boys. We had a gratifying number of leaders of college classes and of Phi Beta Kappa men.

The curriculum, which in the beginning consisted of preparation for college examinations, broadened steadily and took on much more variety and flexibility. Chemistry and physics, with laboratory work, came in for very vigorous attention. Music and art were not part of the curriculum, but boys were at least exposed to them. I feel ashamed to think of two or three boys who went through school without anybody's suspecting that they had artistic talent, but who proved later that they had real gifts. That could not happen now, nor could it have happened within the last ten years.

I have always valued highly the development that comes from debate, and it has been a matter of extreme gratification to me that so large a part of the School has voluntarily participated in this activity with zeal and ambition. Not only does it train a boy to think on his feet, to face an audience without nervousness, and to arrange his thoughts in logical sequence but, pursued through two or three years, it gives him an exceptional knowledge of the main questions before the world of today.

The introduction of honors courses in certain studies enabled us to overcome to a considerable extent one great defect in American education; that is, the neglect of the bright boy. Eventually a division of pupils into two or three different classes according to ability will, I believe, immensely increase the efficiency of our schools.

In short, we have made great progress toward the attainment of the object of education, the development and training of the whole boy. ■

The library in the early days of the school, now the Harley Roberts Reception Room. In 1930 the library was moved to the newly-constructed Charles Phelps Taft Hall.

The Tower under construction — 1913. The semantics of progress at work: for its first 20 years this area was called the "New Building"; for its second 20, the "Old Building"; it is now (officially at least) called the Horace D. Taft Building, usually shortened to "H.D.T." All of these early photographs of the buildings were taken by William N. Bourne '13 and very graciously given by him to the school.

27

The King

Mr. Taft — "the King" — was the kind of man about whom legends flourished. His own warm, vibrant personality, the public impact of the Taft name, with his brother Will as President of the United States from 1909 to 1913, the spreading fame of his school — all of these served to attract recognition and to provide fertile ground for stories and anecdotes about this magnetic figure and the institution he founded and headed. A typical reminiscence from Richard Hooker '95 is reprinted here.

"Memories Come Flooding Back"
by Richard Hooker '95

To write of Mr. Taft and the early days of the school, as the editor of the Alumni Bulletin has asked me to do, is a welcome task. The memories come flooding back. Through them all, like the recurrent theme of a symphony, is the laugh we all knew so well, whether used in honest guile as the gentlest means of disarming our feeble protests against school discipline, in affectionate ridicule to spur us to better work or in launching one more of that inexhaustible, Lincolnian fund of stories.

The picture of Watertown through the familiar seasons as it was fifty, or nearly fifty, years ago comes quickly to mind, although there was more March mud then than now because there were fewer sidewalks. It is easy, too, to recall the old white school building, which miraculously never burned, and the old fair grounds, across a country road from the site of the Rockefeller field, which used to serve for football and baseball while Mr. Taft looked on — afoot like everyone else because there were no bleachers. So also do the pictures come back of the schoolroom in which hardly forty boys were mustered; of the dining room in which the entire senior class sat at one table with Mr. and Mrs. Taft; of the headmaster's office on the same floor to which one went occasionally in response to disciplinary summons but which one remembers better, and likes better to remember, as the scene of inspired and delightful talks. Yet, vivid as all these recollections are, one thing for a time has baffled me.

In the spring of that same year the school had a great religious experience, if the proportions of a conversion from one denomination to another are to be the measure. On a hot Sunday in May a common impulse seemed to lead most of the school down into the meadows below the town where there was a swimming hole that then seemed ideal but which actually may not have been quite that. Nor is it certain that the diving and swimming would have seemed any more ideal to Coach Kiphuth of Yale. But the main purpose was achieved, everybody got wet and there was probably some audible indication of extreme satisfaction with life on the way back through the town. At least Mr. Taft, anxious that the new school should not become a nuisance, thought we had made too much noise and announced that swimming on Sunday was out.

Thereupon Rev. Herbert Cunningham, rector of the Episcopal church, having heard of the edict, hastened to the school with strides shorter only than those of Mr. Taft. He pleaded that if we went to church, his or any other, on Sunday morning we ought to be allowed to go swimming Sunday afternoon. Mr. Taft listened and relented. He explained to the school who had been the intercessor. Somehow it struck the school that that was real religion, revealed from on high. Previously there had been a division in the school between Episcopalians and Congregationalists. By the next Sunday all were Episcopalians — except one and I am not quite sure about the one.

Ten years from the time I came to Watertown fortune sent me to Washington where as a newspaper correspondent I had the privilege of seeing Theodore Roosevelt and William H. Taft at close range. Once when I was permitted to discuss some matter with them both in President Roosevelt's office Roosevelt turned to his secretary of war and chosen successor and asked: "How do you think that schoolmaster brother of yours up in Connecticut, that keeper of your conscience, would feel about this?" It has seemed to me ever since that that phrase was a peculiarly graphic characterization of Mr. Taft and the part he played in the lives of hundreds of those who had been under him. He was the keeper of their conscience in that they tried to set their compass of private living and public service by his high code.

The tall, beloved figure that walks with familiar stride on to the stage thus set by treasured memories, has seemed, at first, too closely identical with Mr. Taft as the school and all the rest of us have known him in recent years. He has seemed, for a time, too nearly the exact man whom one has seen on late visits to the school or while enjoying the hospitality of his home and of delightful hours spent in reminiscing of the old days or in talk of the new battles he was planning to get Connecticut, or the world itself, ordered and governed as he knew it ought to be.

It seemed as if imagination, although equal to the task of a little retrospective makeup and of restoring their earlier color to that white, hussar mustache and white hair, had somehow failed in reproducing the younger man of those golden years. And then the truth dawned! It was the authentic figure of both periods because in the essential qualities of a great personality Mr. Taft had never changed. There was incredibly little difference between the man the

school knew until just a few days ago and the man we knew fifty years ago. Sir Galahad never grew old, nor did "The King."

One of the best remembered episodes is of a night after the last football game of the season. It was an unbeaten team, but I shudder to think what would have happened to it against one of the Taft teams of today. Tom Maffitt would have held his own but, I am afraid, no one else. The reason that I was allowed to play the other guard was that Erastus Tefft conveniently had the mumps. His case became doubly convenient when there arrived for him, just as the last game was being played, a prodigious hamper of things to eat — forbidden of course in these days — which included pheasant, cake and fruit. Such food was not for him! From the isolation hospital, hopefully and successfully established on a rear corridor, he sent word that the hamper was to be turned over to me. So the team assembled in my room that night and our teeth were ecstatically busy when there came a knock at the door.

The answer to drive away pestiferous callers in those days was "meeting." "Meeting" called the team with a unison that would have made any play click on the field. Again a knock and again "Meeting!" Then came a deep, familiar voice with a chuckle in it: "Hadn't you better let me in?" Once in, he draped himself across the bed between two others. But there had been a pause in the business which had been going forward before he knocked. The pause continued until with another chuckle he asked: "Well, aren't you going to give me anything to eat?" I doubt if the school has had better football banquets than that one. ∎

Unforgettable Taft Characters Circa 1912-13

by Anthony Anable '16

The cover photograph on the "Schoolmaster" pamphlet, repeated on the second page of *The Taft Alumni Bulletin* for March 1960, depicts the unforgettable characters who composed the faculty when I reported to the School as a callow 15-year old Lower Middler in September 1912. That same photo appeared, first, in the "Papyrus" that school year and again in the 1913 "Taft Annual."

What a group of colorful, highly original personalities they turned out to be! Forty-eight years later my recollection of them is as clear and vivid as if it were only yesterday. They left their own particular, highly individualistic stamps on all the boys who received a tough, factual education under their relentless efforts in the halcyon years just preceding World War I. They hailed from: Yale, 6; Harvard, 3; Middlebury (Vt.), 3; and Western Reserve, 2. It is hard to believe that in 1912-13 their average age was only 35.

The classroom atmosphere was strict and rugged. The major emphasis was definitely on memorizing and absorbing innumerable hard facts. College Board examinations no doubt influenced this attitude. But College Board exams really presented no obstacles to the boy who had received the coveted recommendation of his master to take them. These recommendations were not easily secured. The masters had a high opinion of the grades made in the College Boards by their students and only recommended those whom they knew would pass creditably with honor to their teachers and their School.

One English master required a written exam each day on the reading assignment, stating "I want a few definite details to show you have read and absorbed the day's assignment." Another, at the end of the school year in Plane Geometry, gave each boy a set of cardboard sheets with over 100

The 1913 FACULTY. Front row, l. to r: Messrs. C.B. Weld, Welles, Roberts, Taft, Welton, G.M. Weld, Ward. Rear row, McIntosh, Hobart, Wilson, Morton, Dallas, Bacon, and Joline.

World War I — Student officers of Taft's ROTC. Ten Taft graduates were killed in the war; five of the ten were aviators who died in aerial combat. Two (Houston Woodward '15 and Stuart Walcott '13) were members of the famed Lafayette Escadrille, and both were awarded the Croix de Guerre with palm.

geometric theorems illustrated and numbered. For the final two weeks we were required to recite word for word each theorem as its number was called, from "given," through "to prove" and, finally, to "Q.E.D." Still another, not content with getting us to the point of reciting the names and dates of the kings of England from 1066 on, actually required us to do it in reverse order from 1914 back to 1066.

I imagine things have changed greatly since then and rightly so. However, we thrived on it. And it was splendid mental discipline that stayed with us all our lives. A thing was right, or it was wrong; there was no middle ground for dispute. Somehow we survived the mental ordeal and acquired what I have often referred to as "a humility in the face of the truth."

In spite of the rigorous, unyielding classroom atmosphere, there existed quite a close and warm relationship out of class between us boys and our masters.

Perhaps that was due to the amazingly high ratio of one master for every ten boys. More probably it was fostered by the colorful personalities of the members of the teaching staff which drew young men to them. We knew them well and they us, and the net result was very good indeed.

Mr. Harley Roberts (Latin) organized a Junior-Lower Middle Club that met Sunday evenings in his quarters to discuss current events and engage in a juvenile type of debating, followed by cider and cookies. Mr. Garfield M. Weld (Mathematics), a crack shot with a rifle or shot gun, used to gather together a group of us at the old fair Grounds for instruction in firearms, which led later to his organizing a gun club. Mr. John Dallas (Religion), a great walker, often took a dozen or more boys on a Sunday, after-church hike to Woodbury and lunch at the Curtis House. All of us who had to endure tutoring at the Weld

Thomas Chrystie '21 managed to graduate not only from Taft but also from Columbia and subsequently became a trustee of both institutions. His son, Tom, Jr., '51 followed in his father's footsteps at Taft and at Columbia, and also became a trustee of both institutions. A third generation, Tom's daughter Adden, graduated from Taft in 1976.

THE TAFT SCHOOL,
WATERTOWN,
CONNECTICUT.

March 8, 1919

MAR 10 1919 REC'D

My dear Mr. Chrystie:

I regret very much to have to send a letter of warning for Tom. Our penalties are given in the shape of demerits. When a boy has fifteen demerits he is put on bounds, that is, is not allowed to go away from the school grounds; when he has thirty a letter of warning is written home to his parents; for fifty he is put on final probation, and for fifty-three is suspended for four weeks. He may subtract from his demerits by going without any for a week, which takes off two; a second week takes off four, a third week in succession takes off eight, etc. Tom has received thirty-three demerits. I will see him today and I feel confident that he will do his best to reduce the number of demerits.

I hope that I shall not have to trouble you again on the subject.

Sincerely yours,

Horace D. Taft

Mr. T. Ludlow Chrystie
19 Cedar Street
New York, N. Y.

brothers' summer camp at Lake Clear, N.Y., got to know informally the tutors — Messrs. Wells, Wilson, Thomas, and, of course, the two Welds, Garfield and Charles. Once at least each year, each boy dined with Mr. Taft. Messrs. Welton and Morton were very popular with all of us through their active coaching of football, baseball, track, basketball, and ice hockey at all levels from the first team down to the Reds and Blues, the little fellows' clubs.

Let me now turn to the teaching staff of those bygone days whose faces peer out at me from the picture in the current *Taft Alumni Bulletin.* They set the atmosphere, intellectually and otherwise, and perhaps I may be excused if I dwell on the more vivid "otherwises." The intellectual atmosphere was very high, as shown year after year by the records we youngsters made in the College Board exams and carried on to our colleges, chiefly Yale as now. Let's have these colorful characters step out of the picture and pass in review, as I call off some of my favorite recollections of them.

Charles B. ("Beanie") Weld (English) was a newcomer to Taft that fall: quiet, kind, but possessed of an ironic sense of humor that in later years approached that of his elder brother, Garfield, whose quaint sense of humor and biting sarcasm became legendary. Charles ("The French-man") Wells (French and German) was a taskmaster and perfectionist of the first water. A "complimentary" final mark of 60 from him in French made me eligible for the diploma I had long before despaired of earning, due solely to my inability to handle modern languages. Never will I forget a term exam just before Christmas vacation, 1915, which he marked 65 and passing, only

to down-grade it to 50 and failing because he also marked the final passage, which was an error-filled attempt of mine to wish Mr. and Mrs. Wells a Merry Christmas and a Happy New Year in French.

Harley Roberts (Latin) was a power-house of energy who seemed to regard the reason for his presence on earth as a mandate to drive Latin into the dull heads of Taft boys by every means at his disposal. This he did with zest and obvious satisfaction. He was not only one of the country's great Latin scholars and Mr. Taft's closest associate, but also a vigorous and excellent teacher. Year after year from "Fabulae Faciles," through Caesar, Cicero, and Virgil, there was no escape from him. If a boy dozed in class, a well-aimed piece of chalk or a blackboard eraser brought him abruptly to his senses. If failing marks and long afternoon detentions didn't inspire in us the will to learn, we were then required to recite each day's assignment in advance during his 6:30 A.M. special (and solitary) breakfast, half an hour before the regular School breakfast. No breakfast, however, for us — just Latin and more Latin until finally we mastered it.

Next in the front row is Mr. Taft, the "King" as we called him. I'll pass him by now, to return to him later. On Mr. Taft's left sits Paul ("Pop") Welton (Athletics) who sometimes filled in for Junior and Lower Middle Latin and English. He "doubled in brass" to cover all sports. Football, and especially baseball, were his favorite dishes. He had won his "Y" in both of them. I well remember how critically he inspected the new boys each fall to detect latent athletic talent. He used to say he could

After Mr. Taft abandoned his plans to build the "new" school on his 300 acres on Nova Scotia Hill, he returned to the original site on Woodbury Road. It is an interesting commentary on the architectural philosophy of the times that the building designed by Cram, Goodhue and Ferguson for the Nova Scotia Hill site (with its fine view) could be moved without change to the level building site in the heart of Watertown. The photo shows the Horace D. Taft Building under construction, with the Warren House clearly visible behind it. Photo taken Oct. 28, 1912.

tell a good baseball player simply by the rakish angle at which he wore his cap. And if a new boy showed up with a baseball cap cocked jauntily over one ear, he had practically made the team.

Garfield M. ("G.M.") Weld (Mathematics) was the most colorful of the lot, and I, as a scientific major, had a full three years of him. Up to that time he had never had a single boy whom he had recommended for a College Board fail. He made it very clear indeed to me, upon giving me his recommendation, what he would do to me and my class-mates if we broke his record. Actually, to his delight, I got 100's in both solid geometry and trigonometry and later successfully weathered four years at M.I.T.

But before that, the going with "G.M." had been tough. Once, before a geometry class he had said to me, "Anable, if your brains were birdshot, there wouldn't be enough to load a flea's shotgun." Another time when I was floundering in trig, he said his five-year old son, Robert, knew more about it than I did. To prove it, that evening at dinner, in the presence of Mrs. Weld and their two young children, Hazel and Robert, he asked me to give him the cosine of an angle, say 37°30'15". After I had given up, he asked Robert, who promptly came up with the correct answer to four decimal places.

One year the standard lunch on Mondays was a huge pile of mashed potatoes, garnished with small pork sausages and brown gravy. "G.M." detested potatoes in any form, especially the mashed variety. For several Mondays we at his table paid little attention

The Biology Lab in the 1930s. Located under the "old" dining room, the area was first used as the school auditorium and stage; then, shown here, as a Biology Laboratory with instructor Robert Olmstead. It is now a maintenance and storage area.

For many years the fall Football Dance was the social event of the year. Here is the 1924 version.

1920 – Vacation Time?

to his muttering, "Hebrews 13:8, Hebrews 13:8." Finally, however, I asked him one Monday what he meant. "Look it up in the Good Book," he replied with a grin. Next day I told him I had consulted the Bible but still failed to understand. "What does the Bible say, Anable?" he asked. I replied, "Jesus Christ, yesterday, today and for ever more." "That's right," he said, "but you've got the accent all wrong; it's on the first two words."

"G.M." also had a famous stunt when a boy stuttered or wavered in his recitation. He would look the boy sternly in the eye; then, with the tip of his tongue, force two false teeth out between his lips. Then, opening his lips, the teeth would pop back into place with a resounding snap that would scare any further recitation out of the boy. Great guy, "G.M."! Pretty raw and uncouth in dress and speech, but a first class math teacher. I'll never forget him, or his dog "Mutt," who he repeatedly said was smarter than any boy at Taft.

C.H. ("Pimp") Ward (English), so nicknamed because of his diminutive stature, five feet plus a couple of inches, was the greatest perfectionist of them all

and a staunch advocate of pure English and correct spelling. At the first session of each new class he outlined forcefully with visual aids his pet dislikes and the penalties that would come to all who failed to avoid them.

The word "Story" was one of them. "There is no such thing," he stated. We would be concerned in this, he added, only with novels, plays, poems, biographies, etc. — *never* with stories. Penalty for using this hated word: 25 percentage points on a 100 percent scoring base. Then on the blackboard he would write the "EI," "IE," words: "weird," "either," "neither," "receive," "deceive," etc. Penalty for misspelling one: 20 percentage points. Finally, using a step ladder, he filled the blackboard from top to bottom with a gigantic "A." Then, in very small letters, he preceded the letter "A" with "sep" and followed it with "rate." "The word is sep-A-rate, *not* sep-E-rate," he would shout. Penalty: 100 points or zero on any written material, however good otherwise, which bore this misspelling. One day Mr. Ward said, in effect, to our class, "Boys, a most wonderful thing has happened. One of your classmates has achieved the all-time low score in a Taft theme: 80 below zero. Young master Anthony Anable has somehow contrived, in an otherwise excellent theme, to misspell 'separate' once, 'weird' twice, and 'neither' and 'receive' once each for a total penalty of 180 points. It is simply incredible, I can't conceive of how he could have done it."

Turning now to the back row, the first master on the left is Mr. Andrew Duncan ("The Mac") McIntosh whose forte was History. No chance to get by unprepared in his five-boy, hour-long class in English History. It was marvelous

CLASS A — TRUSTEES

Horace Taft and Harley Roberts turned over the direction of the school to a Board of Trustees, which first met on December 4, 1926. At this time, "the entire property of the school" was transferred to the new Board pictured above. Not pictured were the five Class B, or Alumni Trustees: Bartow Heminway '17, Elmore McKee '14, Heminway Merriman '97, Thomas Day Thacher '99 and Frederick Wiggin '99.

John H. Goss   Harley F. Roberts   Clarence W. Mendell
Radcliffe Heermance   Horace D. Taft   Arthur Reed Kimball
Irving H. Chase   William H. Taft   Terrence F. Carmody

experience, although it was one of the hardest courses for me. Our Anglo-Saxon heritage came to life under a gifted scholar who combined rare teaching ability with strict discipline, an orderly mind and a great sense of fairness. I was not surprised when, many years later, he became Dean of the School.

Mr. Hobart, "Snecky" as he was known among us boys, taught German, and lived with his wife in a small cottage off campus. I knew him hardly at all, having no courses with him, but those who did admired him greatly. We dedicated our 1916 Taft Annual to Mrs. Hobart to his great delight. Mr. Wilson,

alias "The Bull Moose," taught Math and Physics and was another master I knew only slightly, as was also the case with Mr. Bacon (Latin), and Mr. Joline (Greek). How Mr. Wilson got the nickname, "Bullmoose," I am not certain. However, he does somehow resemble one in the 1913 picture, and he had the habit of trumpeting like one when enraged by a stupid answer to a question. The fact probably was that in the midst of staunch Republican supporters of William Howard Taft to succeed himself for a second term as President, Wilson alone was a Teddy Roosevelt man and an active member of the short lived Bullmoose party of 1912.

Sidney ("Sid") Morton (Latin) was one of the most popular masters in those days. He had won his "Y" in football at Yale and knew a lot about baseball, basketball, and track, in all four of which sports he was a fine coach and assistant to Mr. Welton. He liked boys and spent a lot of his free time with them. He was a true leader and one of the strong men around Mr. Taft. John ("The Dalleye") Dallas (Religion) was then, or shortly thereafter became, assistant headmaster. Eventually he left Taft, resumed his pastoral duties, and finally became Bishop of New Hampshire. He was a tremendous man in the pulpit. His sermons were magnificent and ideally adapted to a congregation of teenaged boys. Under his tutelage, the religious life at Taft thrived, and the T.S.C.S. (Taft School Christian Society) became a real force for good under the presidencies of such outstanding boys as

Bingham Auditorium (1930). Messrs. McIntosh and Thomas preside at Vespers.

Elmore McKee and Charles P. Taft II, Mr. Taft's nephew.

On Mr. Dallas's left is Mr. Bacon (Latin) whom I knew slightly and who left Taft the following year. Last is Olin Coit ("The Greek") Joline (Greek) under whom we science majors had no courses. He was a quiet, rather taciturn, severely dressed, gentleman of the "old school" and was held in the warmest, personal esteem by the few classical majors who studied Greek under him. My chief recollection of him was when, in the absence of the headmaster and other masters senior to him, Mr. Joline was called upon to say Grace before a meal. Even after four years, I was unable to decipher what he said, except for the final "Amen." The words came tumbling out of his mouth in high staccato notes close after one another like a burst from a machine gun. It wasn't Greek, but it sounded like Greek to me and my contemporaries.

I have purposely saved our beloved headmaster, Mr. Taft, until the end. We, among ourselves, called him "The King" and that he most certainly was in every good meaning of the word. Physically (6 ft. 4 in.) and intellectually he towered head and shoulders above the members of his faculty. A shy, humble, and modest man, still mourning the loss of a devoted wife, he was a bit apart, as he should be, from the noisy, rampant school life about him. We boys were somewhat awed by him, and held him on a high pinnacle of honor, character, wisdom, and complete fairness — all the attributes that made up the man each of

us hoped someday to be. He quietly exerted a tremendous influence on all of "his boys" — also on their mothers whom he captivated. As the senior preparatory school headmaster of the country, he also exerted a tremendous influence on the whole course of secondary school education in the United States.

My most vivid recollections of him are some of the impromptu talks he delivered at Sunday evening vesper services, if there were not to be an outside speaker. Standing erect in his habitual dark grey or blue suit, low stiff collar, bright red neck tie, huge gold watch chain, and high black boots, he would address us earnestly on such basic virtues of manhood as "Gumption," "Stick-to-it-iveness," "Being as good as one's word," "Standing up for the right," "Responsibilities of the Privileged Class," etc. And those messages struck home. I, for one, will never forget

some of them or his dramatic references to the poem "Horatio at the Bridge," the man who stood up for what he believed was right, or the essay, "Carrying the Message to Garcia," the young officer who carried out his orders without question and was as good as his word and a paragon of stick-to-it-iveness. His favorite hymn was "Now the Day is Over." We sang it every Sunday evening for my four years at Taft.

He was a staunch believer in a man's right to his personal property. An incident in the fall of 1915 comes to mind. At a Sunday evening assembly, Mr. Taft announced that he had received a phone call from a farmer on the Middlebury Road that his apple orchard had been raided that afternoon by four boys wearing red and blue sweaters. He then added that he was going to his study and would the four boys who were responsible report to him there at once.

Four boys, myself included, followed in his footsteps, feeling secure in the belief that since we were about to fess up to it honestly, we would get off with nothing more than a mild reprimand.

White sidewalls on a new convertible — what more could you want in 1936?

Relaxing at the Senior House with bridge, pipes, and cigarettes — 1936.

The Martin Infirmary (1927), named in honor of Dr. James B. Martin, school physician for 40 years, but more familiarly known in later years as "Grant's Tomb" in honor of Catherine Grant, R.N., shown at right in the photo. In 1971 it was converted to a girls' dormitory and renamed McIntosh House.

Nothing of the kind. We were given such a lecture as we had never heard before until we felt as though we had let down "The King," the School, and our fellow students by an almost criminal offense. Then for good measure, he gave us each 15 demerits, which put us on bounds and in the hard-seated study hall for weeks.

The point I wish to make is this. Mr. Taft lived up to his beliefs, was as good as his word and courageously meted out the punishment that he believed was our due. The fact that we had admitted our guilt was beside the point; he expected nothing less from a Taft boy. A lesser man would have done less, but not "The King." We respected him for it. I don't recall a single word of complaint or criticism from any of us.

Such were the days, as I remember them, in the ancient Warren House with its hard-benched study hall and dining room on the first floor and an old bowling alley leading to a duplex frame building with several small class rooms. The masters and their families lived on the second floor surrounded by an ornate second floor porch of mid-Victorian vintage. We boys, except the youngest who were quartered in the Annex across the road, were scattered through the old hotel rooms on the third and fourth floor. Showers, washrooms, and fire escapes were unknown. Spartan simplicity was fostered by china wash bowls and china water pitchers which often froze solid in winter. Physical fitness and agility of a high order were required to master a contrivance of ropes, pulleys, straps, and fittings provided by the school so that in case of fire one might lower oneself to doubtful safety below.

The breaking of ground in 1913 for what was to be the "new building" (now the old building) sounded the death knell of life as we lived it in the old Warren House. Nostalgic recollections of the simple life there still remain. And the fact that all of my nostalgic recollections of that era are good and have stood the test of time is due in no small part to that heterogeneous group of fourteen unforgettable characters who comprised the Taft School Faculty in 1912-13. ∎

Civics and Debating — Mr. Taft's Special Interests

Mr. Taft's interest in preparing his boys to make a lifetime contribution to their country was evidenced from the start. He taught a class in "Civil Government" himself, a class whose aim was to acquire "an elementary but very useful knowledge of the structure of the government, the main principles of the federal constitution, and the workings of different kinds of local government." The school catalog for 1898-99 concludes the description of the course with these inspiring words: "This class recites every day... There is the freest discussion of all topics connected with politics and the duties of citizenship. The intention is that every pupil who leaves the school shall know as much of what a good citizen should know as a boy of eighteen or nineteen can comprehend, but especially that he shall feel such interest and sense of duty in regard to the subject as will lead him in college and elsewhere to prepare himself thoroughly to do his part in the state patriotically and intelligently."

As a corollary to his interest in what today would be called "participatory democracy," Mr. Taft also had a life-long conviction that debating was an invaluable tool for developing the mind and strengthening a student's (and a citizen's) ability to take an active role in the government of his country, city, or state. Again, the catalog for 1898-99 offers ample evidence of the importance Mr. Taft attached to this area of education. About half of the boys of the school participated in the debating society and, although membership was voluntary, nearly all of the upper class boys were members. The Headmaster himself "presides at the meetings, criticizes the debates and assists the debaters in their preparation."

The debate topics of the early days provide an interesting historical record of the vital issues of the times and also serve to illustrate how much progress has been made since those days. From 1898 to 1905, for example, some of the topics were:

That the Chinese should be excluded from the United States.

A memorable snow sculpture of "The King" — created during his last winter as Headmaster.

The 1935 faculty — Mr. Taft's last year.

That the Hawaiian Islands should be annexed to the United States.

That the United States was justified in going to war with Spain.

That Woman Suffrage is practical and beneficial. (One of the Negative debaters asserted: "Women are easily influenced and, as the whole world knows, they can't keep a secret." The Negative won!)

That the Negroes should be deprived of the right to vote.

That foreign powers should continue to send missionaries to China.

That the English were justifiable in their treatment of the Boers.

That the Senate should be elected by the People.

That the American People were wise in preferring Theodore Roosevelt to Alton B. Parker.

The School's interest in and commitment to debating persisted for many years and was skillfully overseen in more recent days by English master Roland Tyler, who was at Taft from 1925 to 1963.

Even at the end of his career — in his retirement — Mr. Taft, responding to the invitation of Paul Cruikshank, conducted a Civics class with Seniors twice a week.

Days of Youthful Idealism — (And of Schoolboy Insanity)

The foremost impression one takes away after a study of the early days of the school is of the idealism that seems apparent in the major aspects of school life. I am sure there were cynics and scoffers in those days — as always —but they certainly had a low profile, at least in the printed materials of the day: *The Papyrus, The Annual, The Oracle.*

The appeal of idealism was manifest in many ways and in great strength. Week after week the students were exhorted to live a life governed by high ideals and to maintain high standards of personal honor and integrity. They were inspired by some of the most prominent preachers in the land: The Reverend Henry Hallam Tweedy of Yale Divinity School, William Lyon Phelps of the Yale English Department, Alfred E. Stearns, Headmaster of Andover, and many others, whose sermons are reproduced word for word on the front pages of the *Papyrus.* In addition to these "outside" speakers, School Chaplain Arthur Howe provided on-the-scene guidance to the finer way of life. And of course Mr. Taft was a role model without peer.

Reading the sermons today, one is struck by the confident, positive tone: there is no doubt that good will be rewarded and bad punished, sooner or later, one way or the other. A young man who takes the wrong turn early in life ends by dying a sordid, degrading death or by finally repenting after "seeing the light." The good man will also die, but he dies heroically, saving the life of a young girl in a capsized boat, or leading a heroic charge on the battlefield. Stories from the Bible are constantly retold, each illustrating the way a young man can strive to improve his moral fiber.

In addition to formal sermons from adults, editorials by the students' own peers chastised the "fellows" for lapses in behavior at football games or in the dining room and study hall. Letters from alumni exhorted the undergraduates to uphold the honor of the school — to fight the good fight —to continue to struggle even in a losing cause — to bear defeat gracefully and to be generous in victory. Comments from opposing coaches stress how well Taft boys behaved.

Elmore McKee '14 returned to the school to give a Vespers talk: "Taft gave me a vision of a great ideal that grew to be a part of me...the desire to live a life as near Christ's as possible."

A *Papyrus* editorial: "Once a Taft man, always a Taft man...Taft is on trial during the vacation...Let's keep her standard high!...Taft men are gentlemen."

The Mandolin Club was extremely popular in the early days (this illustration from 1906) and persisted through the early 1920s before giving way to the Band Moderne in the '30s.

THE ORACLE

VOL. XXII   FEBRUARY, 1927   No. 4

The Oracle

For 46 years — from 1906 to 1952 — the Oracle filled an important role as an outlet for the creative energy bubbling up in the school. The 1927 masthead of Taft's literary magazine shows a notable editorial board — among them, Maynard Mack '27, later a distinguished professor of English at Yale; Herman Liebert '29, who became Head of the Beinecke Rare Books Library at Yale; Seldon Bacon '27, Professor of Sociology at Yale; and Richard Jackson '29, publisher of the New Haven Register.

Another editorial: "It is for each and every one of us this summer to overcome our several weaknesses and keep Taft's name clear and bright."

Hotchkiss football coach Otto F. Monohan after a 12-0 Hotchkiss victory: "Each side fought a hard game, and the playing was clean. We appreciate very much the sportsmanship and the courteous treatment we always receive here."

Papyrus articles during the war on alumni killed in action: "Frost died with a smile on his face." "Sweeny did not die in vain."

This cannot all be "window dressing." And the few memoirs we have from those days seem to bear out the belief that a high moral tone — a fine sense of values — did in fact prevail. Younger boys looked up to the seniors and tried to behave well to win the approbation of the older "men." Although there were — as always —occasional exceptions, the faculty too seemed worthy of their hire: they were stern, demanding, but fair and understanding when the need arose.

Year after year Harley Roberts led a campaign in support of the George Junior Republic in Litchfield, raising impressive sums of money from the students and the faculty, and reminding the school of the privileges they enjoyed and of their duty to help less fortunate youngsters.

For many years the school sponsored and actively ran a summer camp for poor boys from New Haven. Taft seniors served as counselors and advisors and testified to the worthiness of the endeavor.

In the school itself the Taft Christian Association was a prestigious organization. Election as President was virtually on a par with election as President of the Senior Class.

To balance all the above without, however, detracting from any of the basic substance, it must be demonstrated that schoolboy humor did on one or two occasions put the idealism of the times in perspective with a delightfully wicked satirical issue of the *Papyrus* entitled: "The Graft Perspirus" (5 June 1925).

A glance at the headlines gives some of the flavor:

(The 1927 edition was "The Daft Perspirus".)

Loomus Track Team Bows Very Low to Graft
Graft overwhelmingly defeated the Loomus cracked team by the huge score of seven times the square root of 3 to pi r square.
Gunmen Outgun Gunnery Gunmen
Heartless Graft men smash Pigeons with Abandon.
Big Tea Dance With The Leftover Girls

Even Chaplain Arthur Howe was not immune:

Howl Shoots Wicked Sermon
Except ye renounce Victrolas ye can in nowise enter the Kingdom of Heaven...Fellows, I want to waste a little of your time on this bright and shining Sabbath day by elaborating on that modern engine of iniquity, the Victrola.

An "Iditorial" on "fool Spirit:"
"How can we have organized horseplay and concentrated jeering unless we show the old fool spirit."

A thrust at school rules shows that some subjects are eternally fair game:
No boy who is ill will be allowed in the infirmary until he is nearly dead. No boy who is well shall be allowed out of the infirmary until he is nearly dead.
New regulation for Final Exams: All boys must have their fingernails pulled out, so that nothing can be written thereon.
No boy shall be allowed to wear cuffs.
Boys taking Latin are not to wear rings bearing the school motto.
Boys taking Greek are not to have anything in the room which is Greek to them.
Boys taking Bible are not to pray during the examination.
Boys taking Astronomy must not look out the windows.

But the very next week tradition (or sanity) returned:
To the outgoing Seniors: "...all kinds of good fortune in their work ahead at college and to express a sincere hope that they will carry all through their lives a deep appreciation for what this school has done for them and a love for Mr. Taft and the school that will never die."
On the coming summer vacation:
"Wherever we go the consciousness of being Taft men will be in our minds...We have a responsibility to live up to the standards of the school...Every failing of ours, every little or mean act directly affects the school's reputation."

EXTRA   EXTRA

THE GRAFT PERSPIRUS

VOL. XXXII.   WATATOWN, CONN., JUNE 5, 1925.   No. 30.

GRAFT DEFEATS CHOKE, 3-2

Choke Beaten by Graft, 2-3

WINNERS VANQUISH LOSERS, 3-2

Visitors Fail to Overcome Opponents, 2-3

The Graft basketball nine vanquished the Choke aggregation, losing by the score of 2 to 2, last Sunday in the lecture hall. Our boys led by a large margin throughout, trailing far behind the visitors till the last few minutes. The Choke teamwork was terrible, and their players worked together perfectly.

Captain Courageous started the scoring for the visitors, making three runs in the first lap. Bloke, of Choke, then won three straight rubbers, but was stymied on the sixth green by Joke, two up and three to go. Bill trumped Alf's ace, and was layed low for the count of ten. The round ended, score 7 to 5.

Captain Inamessovitch started things going for Graft by bowling three men in quick succession. Lillian Russell parried the thrust, however, and went two no trump. But stay; General Custard was on hand. Once more he fired, and another redskin bit the dust. Edwards shot two fowls on the wing. His faithful dog Nina retrieved them. Miss Bronson tore off five yards around left end. After some clever broken field running by Fowler, the semi-colon ended, 0 to 0.

With the ball on Yale's 80-yard line and with 4 3-5 seconds to go, our fellows tried a forward pass. The pellet rolled around the cup for an agonizing moment, and then fell in with a loud crash. The game was ours; Spring had gotten a fall.

The outstanding players of the game were Snitz for Graft, and Snitz, who starred for the visitors: The lineup:

We		They
A. Fool		Helas
	East Wind	
D. Fool		P. Lund
	Dealer	
Eheu		A. Pig*
	Piano	
Mopsa		B. Pig
	Cornet	
Sopsa		Sopy
	"It"	
Flopsa, Digestion		
	Extras	

*This little pig went to market.

Substitutions: Yes for no, no for yes, three four five.

Double plays: Diddle to Dum to Diddle to Dum to Diddle to Dum to Diddle.

Referee: Smelly.

GUNMEN OUTGUN GUNNERY GUNMEN

Heartless Graft Men Smash Pigeons with Abandon

Last Saturday the gun team won decisively from the Techee Indian Tribe in the last and most inspiring shoot of the year. T. Wilson was high scorer for Graft with 3 out of 4; however, he was soon obliged to stop because his conscience hurt him. The shoot was made conspicuous by the fact that there seemed to be perfect coordination between the trigger and the firing-pin, the recoil often almost immediately following the detonation. Occasionally one of the Techees carelessly allowed his gun barrel to become bent by too excited shooting; however, few casualties are reported. The complete score is as follows:

Graft
T. Wilson—3 out of 4.
W. Begg—(Killed by 1st shot).
Cheney and S. Cobb—(Frightened away by noise).

Teehee Indians
Chief Standing-Room-Only—5 out of 500.
Chief Mugurump—(Bitten to death by fierce pigeon).
Chief Engineer—(Lost his gun).

REV. GERALD CHAPMAN ADDRESSES T. S. B. S.

Tells School How to Succeed In Life

Last Sunday evening Rev. G. Chapman of Atlanta, Ga., addressed the T. S. B. S. meeting, speaking on a topic that greatly interested his listeners. Mr. Chapman has spent much of his time in the last few years working at a Federal institution at Atlanta, Ga., and before this was connected with another good works at Ft. Leavenworth, Kans. The service opened with the singing of a favorite hymn, "The Bowery; We Don't Go There Anymore," ably led by T. Wilson at the piano. After this Vice-President McCaskey, in the absence of President Symmers, introduced Mr. Chapman, who spoke as follows:

"Fellers," he said, "as soon as I heard youse singing dat hymn I knowed dat here was where my speech ud go big. Where I been working in de last few years, dey don't sing no hymns like dat. Down in de East Side of Oakville there are more than seventeen people that are starving. They can't get work. Just think of that, can't get work to do at all. Now youse boys here don't have to worry about that. You have plenty of work. You have to get up at five o'clock some mornings to do it all, I hear. But down there in Oakville the men and the women and even the boys and girls haven't any work to do at all. They used to (Continued on page 4, column 1.)

CALENDAR

Wednesday
8:30—Flea Club

Thursday
1:45-2:00—First team baseball practice
2:00-5:30—Class team baseball practice

Friday
8:31-11:35—Senile Berating Club

Saturday
4:30—Tea Dance for Leftover Girls

Sunday
8:30—T. S. B. S. Shoot

Monday
8:30—Borem Berating Club

Tuesday
2:36 a. m.—Upper Middle Bed-Dumping Club
11:35 p. m.—The Perspiring Appears

KLOSE KLASS KONTEST KAPTURED BY KORPER'S KLOUTING KRUSADERS

Hector Hits Hilarious Homer

In an exceedingly close and interesting battle the Snotty Senior team blew itself to a victory over the Messy Middlers by the score of 20 to 0. In only eight of the nine innings did the victors fail to cross the plate, and they also played well in the field, cutting short many threatening rallies by sparkling errors. Billy Begg, in the box for the Seniors, was hard beset in the first frame-up, in which the enemy garnered fourteen hits, but by a magnificent exhibition of headwork he prevented any scoring by walking all those who threatened to hit. After the Senior team had committed four triple plays, none of which were counted, since the umpire wasn't looking, the side was retired.

In the fourth round Thorns showed great presence of mind when he allowed a ball which was (Continued on page 5, column 3.)

ROLL ON, HONOR ROLL!

This month the Seniors lead the school in scholarship with an average of 98. O'Day and Graham are tied for first with 100 each, while Gray is a close second with 99 42-42. It is gratifying to note the seriousness of purpose with which even the leaders of the school bluff through their studies. The lineup:

Seniors		
O'Day	100	
Graham	100	
Gray	99 42-42	
Bryant	99 2-39	
Hiestand	98 3-4	
Edwards	98	634567-999999
Begg	95	

et cetera ad absurdum. Limited space prevents our publishing the records of the other classes, which were far inferior.

LOOMUS TRUCK TEAM BOWS VERY LOW TO GRAFT

Williamson Breaks School Record in High Hurdles

Last Thursday morning Graft overwhelmingly defeated the Loomus cracked team by the huge score of seven times the square root of 3 to pi square. Wood starred for Graft in the weight events by throwing the hammer three and one-half furlongs and putting the shot one cubit. In the pole vault Wilson nearly tied the school record with a beautiful vault of seventeen fathoms. D. Smith of Graft starred for Loomus by winning the half mile in the wrong direction. It is altogether probable that Hotchkiss would have won the hundred yard dash if he had not stepped on a piece of chewing gum on the last lap and lost his shoe.

The summaries are as follows:
100-yard dash—Podge, Graft, first; Bitterman, Graft, second. Time 14.4 sec.
220-yard dash—Pale, Graft, first; Podge, Graft, second. Time 27.1 sec.
440-yard dash — Brimstone, Graft, first; Preserves, Graft, second (Continued on page 4, column 3.)

BIG TEA DANCE WITH THE LEFTOVER GIRLS

Assisted by the Tilford Tots' Swimming Team

The charming misses of the Leftover School came here last Sunday at 2 o'clock midnight for a thedansant with a few of our more serpentile members who were ably assisted by the visiting swimming team of the Tilford Tutoring School (nee Rosenkowpulanskibaum). The afternoon was a huge success, as there was but little interference from station Y-A-L-E, broadcasting on all wave-lengths. By the way, we might mention the outcome of the swimming meet with the Tilford Tots. Graft easily defeated her rugged opponents, winning every match but the foursome. They scored a grand slam in the 2-pound shot put, which was their only tally of the morning.

But enough of these frivolous things, and let us return to the fair mademoiselles. They were gorgeous in their green taffeta aprons. The bride wore a—but that's another story. Cold concentrated sulphuric acid was served with sodium cakes. The effect was almost volatilizing. And then the music! Oh, what spirit-ennobling harmony gushed forth from the full-lipped kazoos! Mingled with the soft, cooing strains of the trip-hammer were the weird, sensuous, insidious, gripping, exotic, ethereal, ephemeral, oxidizing, ossifying beats of the soprano cello, which resembled the staccato moans of a nauseated bobo bird. The girls were delightful and showed excellent table manners (Continued on page 4, column 2.)

HOWL SHOOTS WICKED SERMON

"Except Ye Renounce Victrolas Ye Can in Nowise Enter the Kingdom of Heaven"

RECALLS INCIDENT OF COLLEGE DAZE

Criticizes Attitude of United States Senate

"WHATSOEVER A MAN SEWETH THAT ALSO SHALL HE RIP"

Taking as his text, "Forasmuch as we are encompassed about by a cloud of witnesses, it would be better to preach a sermon of our own than to read one of Dean Brown's," the Rev. Sir Arthur Howl, noted athlete, preached a wretched sermon in church last Sunday.

"Fellows, I want to waste a little of your time on this bright and shining Sabbath day by elaborating on that modern engine of iniquity, the victrola. I knew a fellow at college once—alas, poor Brown, I knew him well—who went completely to the bad by playing his victrola at three o'clock in the morning. Instead of entering the ministry as he might have done, he went steadily from bad to worse until he finally became a United States Senator. (Applause.)

"Fellows, I want you to realize that such examples as these show the insidious effect of the victrola. The discordant jazz melody jars the aural nerves connecting with the cerebellum. This produces a distinct agitation of the spine at the ninth vertebra, from which we get acute inflammation of the esophagus, pulmonary embolism, or delirium tremens. Think of it, fellows. It grieves me deeply. When you get to college, tread in the straight and narrow path and keep away from these evils. (Laughter.)

"Fellows, in conclusion, I want you all to volunteer to throw all victrolas into the pond after lunch. If we have two volunteers, it will take an hour, if we have ten it will take two hours, and if we have thirty, I shall faint. Let us sing the chant on page 14,578."

ALUMNI OFFICERS

The officers of the Alumni Association next year are:
President—Ingalls.
Vice President—Husted.
Sec.-Treasurer—Goldsmith.
Executive Committee
To serve until Odell marks at breakfast—E. Richardson, Jimmy Johnson, King.
To serve until a swimming pool is built—N. Smith, Rawl, Carson.
To serve until the infirmary burns up—P. Martin, H. Brown, Ellis.

Two Decades of Growth 1910-1930

From 1910 to 1930 the school experienced a twenty-year period of remarkable growth in every area: student body, physical plant, tuition charges. Interestingly enough, the area of least change was the academic structure.

Thriving in the hospitable educational climate of the times, the school was well established by 1910, but it was still in many ways "Mr. Taft's School." The 1910 catalog made it clear that "The limited number of boarding students makes it possible for the Head Master to be in close touch with each boy." Boarding accommodations were available for 95 boys, although 110 students — including day students — were actually enrolled for the year 1909-1910. Twenty states were represented. Not including Mr. Taft, the faculty consisted of ten men — although Mr. Taft is listed as teaching History and Civil Government. Tuition was $800.

In 1931-32 (the School archives do not have a copy of the School catalog for 1930-31) there were 323 boys from 28 states and France and Japan. Twenty-seven masters are listed, and the catalog reveals the change from "Mr. Taft's School" of 1910 by stating that *all* of the masters now share the responsibility of student supervision: "The number of Masters makes it possible for them to be in close touch with all the boys and for intimate relations to exist between Faculty and students." Tuition for the year 1932-33 was $1,600.

Changes in the physical plant provide as always the most obvious measure of change and growth. In 1910 the Old Warren house was still the main campus building, although the central part of the Annex had been built in 1908. But at the end of the twenty year period the main elements of the present school were essentially in place. The old "Main Building" — now Horace D. Taft Building — was built in 1914, and in 1927 the Infirmary and Service buildings were constructed. (When girls arrived in the 1970s these two buildings were converted to girls' dormitories; they are now McIntosh House and Congdon House.) In 1929 the Old Warren House was demolished to make room for the "new" building, now Charles Phelps Taft Hall, which was still under construction in 1930. The Annex had been enlarged in 1911, and a gymnasium added the same year. Rockefeller Field was constructed in 1922.

In the non-physical area, the most momentous event of the period occurred in 1927 when Mr. Taft and Mr. Roberts, who had jointly owned the school, turned it over to a Board of Trustees, thus making possible the large-scale fund-raising effort that was necessary for the new construction of the late nineteen twenties.

Three stalwart old-time faculty members died during this period: Paul Welton in 1921, Olin Coit Joline in 1925, and Harley Roberts in 1930. The Cum Laude Society was founded in 1922, and three clubs, Alpha, Beta, Gamma were organized in 1930 to replace the Seneca, Cayuga, and Mohawks that had been in action since 1922. The Alumni Bulletin started publication in 1923.

But the central core of the institution remained remarkably unchanged from 1910 to 1930. The commitment to four years of English and Mathematics is common to both years. So, too, was the requirement for four years of Latin. In 1909-10 three years of Greek and two years of a Modern Language were required for graduation. In 1932-33 the language requirement demanded three years of Greek, French, or German. In the earlier period Bible History was required for one period a week for the three Lower classes, while the '32-'33 catalog states merely: "Bible study is required for the three lower classes."

FAIRCHILD AERIAL SURVEY, INC. N.Y.C.

Probably the first aerial view of
the school, about 1925.

Taft Athletics in the Thirties
by Charles H. Shons

1936 Football Team

After a fairly careful review of the whole record, I feel confident that the '30s stand out rather strikingly for many sports in the School's athletic history.

There have been other decades when Taft rose to greatness for prolonged periods in certain sports or when individual teams wound up with a season's record the peer of any for all time. Back as far as the 1890s, Taft teams in ice polo (the forerunner of hockey that took over in 1901) had phenomenal success against redoubtable opponents. I am told that Taft even met the Yale varsity on an even basis in ice polo, a sport now obsolete but which was in its time best characterized as a sport of modified mayhem*. Then, too, some of the basketball teams of the early 'teens, 1913 especially, made outstanding records. Similarly the football, basketball, and golf teams of 1923, the football team of 1925, and the undefeated wrestling team of 1928 are very memorable. No period in basketball has equalled, however, that of the mid-forties, nor has Taft ever had a succession of hockey victories to equal those of the 1950s, the decade which saw Mays Rink built and the assurance of playable ice all winter long. The 1950

League Championship Baseball team and two soccer elevens (one early in the '50s, one late) made remarkable records. The late 1950s soccer eleven took the League Championship and won over Yale Freshmen for the first time in Taft soccer history. But the steady, super-lative performance in four sports in the 1930s put a stamp of athletic greatness on that decade. In my opinion it has not been equalled in any comparable time in Taft's annals.

The period of which I write was sent into high orbit actually in 1931. The football team of the fall of 1930 was the first in that sport in Taft history to play through its schedule undefeated and untied; soccer lost but one out of six games, hockey only one out of five. Wrestling won all but one of its meets in a schedule that included Springfield, Harvard Freshmen, and Andover. (Choate was to be the wrestlers' jinx all through the decade!) Finally, baseball came through its ten games undefeated, a great rarity never achieved before or since in that delicately balanced game. It was a most sensational year for the School in many other respects — the Charles Phelps Taft Building was

50

commissioned for full use, Fathers' Day and the club system were inaugurated. Best of all, there was a fine undergraduate spirit throughout, sparked by a topflight Senior Class.

Football was undoubtedly the stellar performer in the thirties. It went from the 1931 season to be undefeated and untied in three successive years, with a whopping 47-0 victory over Hotchkiss in the fall of 1934. In the fall of 1935 the team had the remarkable record of being undefeated and *unscored on* — though the Loomis game was a 0-0 tie. The next year saw still another undefeated season, with one tie game. In the fall of 1937, football closed its "place in the sun" (i.e., for the decade) with a one-defeat record.

Perhaps the most outstanding success against potent opponents in the 1930s was achieved in wrestling. After the 1931 season previously mentioned, the grapplers lost only to Harvard Freshmen in 1932, downing Springfield and M.I.T. Freshmen and Andover. In 1934 they lost only to Choate in five meets. The next year, however, came the climax: undefeated and untied in a 7-meet schedule that included Wesleyan, Williams, Yale, and Springfield Freshmen and Andover. Choate, that year, *probably* missed defeat by having an epidemic of contagious disease! Again in 1937 the wrestlers went undefeated, and in 1939 closed the ten-year record of greatness by winning seven out of eight meets, including Yale, Williams, and Wesleyan Freshmen and Hotchkiss.

The third consistent victor in the 1930s was the new sport of soccer. It had become a "letter sport" after the undefeated season of 1928-29 and by 1931 (already noted) was playing a schedule comparable in size and difficulty with those of the teams senior to it. In the falls of 1933 and 1934 came two more one-defeat seasons, with the latter ending in successive victories over Loomis, Choate, and Hotchkiss. In

1936-37 there was a strange outcome — one defeat and three ties, one of them with Yale Freshmen. The 1938-39 team won seven out of nine games. Soccer's record for the decade ended brilliantly in the fall of 1939 with a clean sweep of all its opponents (including Wesleyan's J.V.) save one. It met its only defeat at the hands of Yale Freshmen in a heart-breaking overtime 2-1 contest.

Although not quite so *frequently* ultra-successful as other teams, track established a record in the mid-thirties that has never been equalled in Taft history. In 1934 the trackmen lost but one out of five meets; in 1935 only one out of four. In 1936 it "rang the bell" for the first undefeated season in track in the decades I write of, though there seems to have been one such back around 1910. This remarkable result was followed by two years with only one defeat apiece to complete a five-year high watermark for track. ■

---

*This change from ice polo to hockey in 1901 was marked by an unusual and interesting episode. Shortly before his death some eight years ago, the chief actor in it told me about it: Charles ("Hemp") Sherwood, '02, ice polo captain-elect for 1901-02, turned over his captaincy to a newcomer, Roger Alling '03. Alling knew and played ice hockey and could therefore coach and lead Taft's first team in the new sport!

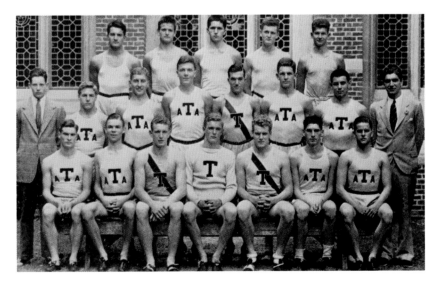

1936 Track Team

PAUL AND EDITH CRUIKSHANK
HEADMASTER 1936—1963

EDUCATION

Taftless Taft

"My victuals still taste good." Horace Dutton Taft jovially assured 300 of his "old boys" at the New York Yale Club last week. Despite that sign of health the brother of the late William Howard Taft was announcing his retirement within the year as headmaster of Taft School.

In a profession studded with Grand Old Men. Headmaster Taft at 73 shares with Groton's Endicott Peabody (TIME, Oct. 28) the distinction of being the grandest of them all. A distinguished, kindly man, "Brother Horace" has the Taft good humor, the Taft chuckle, the flowing Taft

PAUL AND EDITH CRUIKSHANK—*1937.*

International

"BROTHER HORACE" TAFT

His victuals still taste good.

mustache. But because he is six feet six and spare, he looks less like his rotund brother than like that other late great jurist, Oliver Wendell Holmes.

Seven years out of Yale, Horace Taft founded Taft School in 1890, soon housed it in an old hotel at Watertown, Conn. Nourished by the eminence of the Taft name, it grew until by 1914 it was delivering up some 25 boys a year to Yale plus a few to Harvard and Princeton. Headmaster Taft became the idol of his students and got on famously with parents, most of whom smiled at his long devotion to the cause of Prohibition. By 1927 the school ranked among the best in the country and Mr. Taft turned it over to a board of trustees, who shortly raised $2,000,000 for handsome new buildings.

A teacher of the old school, Mr. Taft has always believed in making his boys work hard, giving them heavy doses of Latin and mathematics. Once some progressive educators were urging him to teach the boys to use their hands. specifically to put in a course in milking. "Why," demanded Mr. Taft, "should we teach them to do something which any calf can do better?" Last week he had a fling at the College Entrance Examination Board, currently tinkering feverishly with

its tests in an effort to please progressive teachers. "You would think," observed the old headmaster, "that it had St. Vitus's dance."

Paul Cruikshank's 27 Years

Early in the 1930s it became increasingly apparent that it was time for Mr. Taft to hand over the school to another man. In his own words: "I had been aware for some time that I had been gradually delegating more of my work to others, and that what I had kept for myself was done with less vigor and with more interruptions on account of health." A committee of old boys approached him and urged him to appoint an understudy — a successor. But Mr. Taft felt that the succession question should be undertaken by a committee that would report to the Board of Trustees.

On December 6, 1935, at a dinner at the Yale Club in New York City, Mr. Taft announced that he would resign on July 2, 1936. The search for his successor was quick and fruitful, for as early as February it was announced that Paul Cruikshank would succeed Mr. Taft as the school's second headmaster.

Paul Fessenden Cruikshank was born in Dorchester, Massachusetts, October 1, 1898, one of a family of ten children. He prepared for college at Blair Academy, Blairstown, N.J., and entered Yale in 1916, working his way through college by teaching, coaching, and newspaper reporting. He spent two of his college summers working for steel companies. Although he majored in law and history, he also won two Latin prizes and was appointed to a Junior Oration.

Graduating in 1920, he taught at the Hopkins Grammar School, where he was an instructor in Latin and director of Athletics. In 1922 he moved to the Gunnery School, where he held the same positions until 1930, when he founded his own school, Romford, in Washington, Connecticut. A very

successful school, Romford — and Mr. Cruikshank — seemed to parallel Taft and Mr. Taft — at least in the eyes of the *Papyrus,* which pointed out that after five years Mr. Taft's school had forty students, while Romford at the same age had exactly the same number of students. Furthermore, Mr. Taft and Mr. Cruikshank shared the same interests — history and law.

At the time of his appointment, Mr. Cruikshank was thirty-seven and Mr. Taft seventy-five.

Mr. Taft and his successor — 1936.

"What Can the Man Do Who Comes after the King?"

Alumni Day, May 16, 1936, was of course a memorable occasion. The Hon. Thomas Day Thacher presided as Toastmaster, and Harold W. Dodds, President of Princeton University, was the principal speaker. In his opening remarks, Mr. Cruikshank immediately endeared himself to the audience by making the most gracious, tactful comments he could possibly make by quoting from the Bible: "What can the man do who comes after the king?"

In a courteous gesture that was emulated by Mr. Cruikshank 27 years later, Mr. Taft took himself off to California for a year, allowing his successor to start his stewardship on his own — without "the King" looking over his shoulder. When he returned, he took up residence in the Ashworth House on the Green in Watertown, and continued to have close association with the school, having Seniors to dinner and conducting a class in civics.

Meanwhile, the Cruikshank era seemed off to a good start. In the fall of '36 the school was filled to capacity, and it opened in the fall of 1937 with the largest enrollment in history — 351 students from "nearly every state" and three foreign countries. In its welcoming editorial, the *Papyrus* stated: "On the very first night of school Mr. Cruikshank gave evidence of his charm of personality in an address to the Senior class, an address which instantly won over to him the hearts of the Seniors."

Mr. Cruikshank's twenty-seven year tenure was by no means all smooth sailing. His first year 1936-37, found the school — and the nation — still mired in "The Great Depression." The next four or five years saw a very gradual climb out of the depths, but the economic climate was still not universally healthy when the war years 1941-46 violently changed both the social and the economic picture. In the uncertain aftermath of the war, 1945-50, the school sought to find its place in the vastly different environment of the postwar years. But then, for perhaps ten years, everything seemed to fall into place, and the Headmaster and his school experienced what Joe Cunningham has called the "golden years" — 1951-61. The "turbulent sixties" loomed on the horizon, but were still not actually on stage, and a fresh hand on the helm — John Esty — would have to deal with them. But the nation was prosperous and self-confident, and the school was healthy too, with a full enrollment and a strong faculty.

In 1940 Dance Weekends really were formal. White tie and tails were not confined to Fred Astaire.

Cruikshank Innovations

Although Mr. Cruikshank maintained that he would not "seriously disturb the status quo," changes were, of course, inevitable. One of the first changes in the social climate of the school was the introduction of complete self-government by the Senior Class. In making "unlimited late lights" a privilege for the seniors, the Headmaster stressed his belief in the ability of each individual to "regulate" himself so that he could achieve a satisfactory balance between work and play. Corridor Committees were established so that each dormitory corridor would be supervised by a group of boys (rotated every two weeks) charged with the duty of keeping order during the evening study period: "No master would be in evidence." Every Senior would serve on the Committee at least once. The innovation was greeted enthusiastically by the student body, and later in the year the self-governing privilege was extended to the Upper Middle class.

Actually another "innovation" had been started even earlier in the year, when Seniors were asked to select the hymns to be sung at Sunday night Vespers — a tradition that lasted until the institution of Sunday night Vespers disappeared in the turmoil of the 1960s.

Another early Cruikshank tradition also got its start his first year, when the Christmas Church Service found its form in December 1936. With leadership provided by George and Nora Morgan, this lovely service held in Christ Church again provided an emotionally satisfying close to the fall term until it, too, succumbed to the upheavals of the 1960s. In the early '70s, the Christmas

service was reconstituted and it continues to make an important contribution to the end of term festivities. Looking back, it does not seem like a great change, and yet the idea of letting the boys sleep as late as they wished on the last Sunday morning of the term was a significant change in the highly-structured routine of the day. The usual Sunday morning service at 9:15 was moved to 5:30 p.m., the church was beautifully decorated with Christmas trees and candles, and the program of carols sung by both the choir and the entire student body helped bring the community together in a most satisfying manner.

Mr. Cruikshank's youth and energy were clearly in evidence in these early days. Reading the back issues of the *Papyrus,* one is constantly impressed by how much the Cruikshanks (for Mrs. Cruikshank accompanied him on many of his trips) were "on the go." There were many short trips to New York, New Haven, and Boston, but longer trips were scheduled nearly each term to Chicago, Denver, Minneapolis, the West

Argyle socks, saddle shoes, and bobby socks were much in evidence at Spring Dance Weekend. Boys and their dates watch the baseball game from the stone wall lining Woodbury Road.

Coast — and numerous places in between.

While many of his trips were concerned with alumni affairs, many were also involved with professional matters — the serious business of educating the young. Early in 1937, for example, he was in New York at the 12th annual Conference of the Secondary Education Board, speaking on "Emotional Problems and their Solution." And he was in demand at other schools: he would deliver a sermon at The Harvey School, speak at Loomis and Wooster, attend numerous professional conferences in New York, New Haven, and at one time, the Headmasters' Association in Atlantic City, when he was made a member of that group.

Back in Watertown, he encouraged his faculty to develop their interests and talents for the betterment of the school: The *Oracle* was reestablished under the able guidance of English Instructor William Sullivan. And although drama had long been an important extra-curricular activity at Taft, he saw to it that Biology Instructor Robert Olmstead organized the activity and it was at this time (1937) that the name The Masque and Dagger Society was first used. The tradition of New Boy

Ties was introduced in 1939. In short, there was no question but that a firm hand was in control.

Although the school had a record enrollment in 1937, there were some who felt that a better job could be done with somewhat smaller numbers, and that certain areas of the school were overcrowded — the locker rooms and the dining room, for example. In any case, for a variety of reasons, the decision to reduce the enrollment was made in the Spring of 1940. The former boarding enrollment of 325 was reduced to 300; the total enrollment including day students was 325 in September 1940.

At various times in the '20s, '30s, and '40s the faculty produced a number of skits, farces, and "dramas" for the astonishment and entertainment of the students. Here, from the '40s is the cast of the faculty play, "What Happened to Jones?" — L. to R., Mr. Tyler, Mr. Bartter, Mrs. Fusonie, Mr. Shons, Mrs. Olmstead, Mr. Adams, Mr. Sullivan, Mrs. Adams, Mr. Olmstead, Mr. Fusonie, Mrs. Shons, Mr. Sexton.

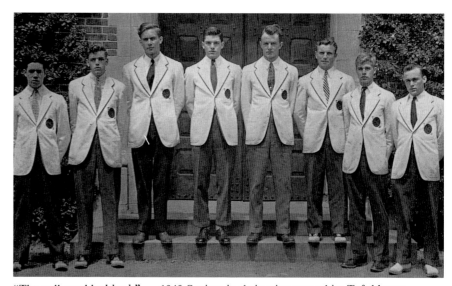

"The well-scrubbed look" — 1940 Seniors in their crisp new white Taft blazers.

A Fuss Over Breakfast

A relatively minor occurrence in the fall of 1940 provides a most interesting contrast between the attitudes of the students at this time and the attitudes of students twenty years later — during the tumultuous '60s. The matter arose over the decision of the administration to eliminate the main course of eggs and bacon at breakfast. The school had recently begun serving a mid-morning lunch, and "the authorities" (as they are referred to) decided that a) the usual breakfast was "too long and of a heaviness that was not really necessary" and b) the expense of the new mid-morning lunch "threw the school's food budget out to the extent of some two or three thousand dollars." By omitting one course from the regular breakfast, part of the cost of mid-morning lunch might be recovered.

The Editors of the *Papyrus* noted that they had been asked to poll the students to obtain their opinion of this change, but they refused to do so on the grounds that such a poll "might stir up discontent and rancor. It appears that a large part of the student body might favor giving up the mid-morning lunch in return for larger breakfasts. But the authorities have already decided that such a move would be unwise. And we must remember that our first duty here at Taft *is to support the school*. The *Papyrus* therefore places itself on record as approving this new measure, and it urges all the members of the student body to lay aside their personal feelings and make up their minds that what has been done has been done for the best."

The contrast between the two eras is marked indeed. The idea that the first duty of the *Papyrus* is "to support the school" would have caused editors of the 1960s to roll on the floor with laughter. It might be nearer the truth to suggest that many of the editors felt just the reverse: that their prime duty was to *expose* areas of (in their view) administrative misjudgment and to press for immediate reform. The idea that "the authorities" know best was anathema to any self-respecting editor from 1960 on.

Another example of the tenor of the times concerned a letter that some unidentified Taft student mailed with the admonition on the envelope: "Handle quickly, Mr. Farley" (then the Postmaster General). The letter was returned to Taft with a covering note from the local Postmaster: "Boys will be boys — I fully realize that. However, they should also have respect for their elders. Therefore, I am returning your letter. Please eliminate your advice to Mr. Farley, as I am 'POSITIVE' he does not need it. The second offense will cause your letter to be turned over to Mr. Cruikshank. Sincerely _____".

The phrase "respect for elders" seems as outdated today (1985) as the buggy whip, and the idea that a local businessman thought that the headmaster could control such an incident is quaint and curious. One might hazard a guess that in the '60s the next day the postmaster would have had two hundred letters *each* marked: "Handle quickly, Mr. Farley."

During World War II, in addition to helping local farmers harvest their apple crops and gathering scrap metal for the "war effort", boys served as air raid spotters, using the Field House as a spotting post. Working in conjunction with the local Civil Defense Committee, the seniors served three-hour night watches during the winter term of 1942.

War Clouds Gather

With Britain and France at war in September 1939, the school, like the nation, began preparing for America's involvement in the struggle. That fall an English student and a German student entered the school, and next year a French refugee came to Taft. A *Papyrus* poll noted that 88% of the students supported the allies, and Mr. Reardon predicted that England would win even if America remained neutral. In what surely must be one of the most clouded crystal balls in history the Taft student body voted 94% for Wendell Willkie in a 1940 straw vote. Sixteen Taft masters were eligible for the draft, and navigation and artillery courses were started in the fall of 1940. A year later, as the guns of war grew ever louder, 37% of the student body felt that the U.S. should go to war with Germany immediately. In October '41 the destroyer Reuben James was sunk, and Taft suffered its first war casualty: Howard Wade '38. By January 1942, students were taking three hour shifts in the Civil Defense, spotting planes in a tower built on Rockefeller Field, and a math master, Jess Hall, left to join the artillery.

By the fall of 1942, the school was thoroughly involved in the war effort. The *Papyrus* noted that "scarcely a detail of school life was not altered by the war." A Commando Training Program replaced the usual calisthenics, and an obstacle course was built on part of the golf course. Students participated in a scrap metal drive, and a shortage of meat and sugar caused changes in the school menus.

At Taft for a Trustees meeting in May 1943, News Commentator Lowell Thomas, father of Lowell, Jr. '42, made his regular weekly Friday night radio broadcast from the stage of Bingham Auditorium. Calling Watertown "one of the most charming small towns in Eastern America," Mr. Thomas praised the training of young men "to represent Uncle Sam all over the world...the present mission of the Taft School."

Introduction of the Job System: Henry Estabrook '43 Recalls the Changes

But the most far-reaching change involved what is now called the Job System. The start of this important aspect of school life is recorded in the next section by one of the students responsible for the successful launching of the job program. Henry Estabrook '43 has provided this thoughtful after-view of his days at Taft during the war years:

"The following is one man's memories of our school when it was influenced by economic and social changes brought about by the war.

"I came to Taft nine months after our country got into the war. Changes in our school came about gradually and were more pronounced in our Senior year. Taft was a strict environment when I was a Middler versus what one would experience certainly today. We wore coats and ties most of the day, the exception being after lunch in the afternoon and evenings if you studied in your rooms. Loafers, moccasins, sneakers were definitely 'outsville'. We did as we were told by the Masters and Upperclassmen. Oh, yes, you well knew it was a male school, not coed until almost twenty-five years later. Each evening there was a Vespers and no one spoke walking to Vespers at Bingham Auditorium. Lining the corridor were the Monitors ready to reprimand you if you spoke a word. Each person had his assigned seat at Vespers. Usually there was a talk by Paul Cruikshank or one of the Faculty, a prayer and then a hymn. Afterward we proceeded to dinner. A blessing was given and then dinner served by waitresses. This was to change in my Upper-Middle and Senior years when the staff left to work in the Waterbury war plants and students took over this duty.

"As a new boy, one of our first tasks, aside from class orientation, etc., was to learn the school's alma mater — "Oh Kind Firm Molder of a Thousand Boys," which I learned was written by John Knox Jessup, an earlier alumnus and later to be one of *Time* magazine's prestigious editors. Each new boy was assigned an Old Boy to help the former get acclimated at school. . . .

"A student always addressed a Master as "Mr." or "Sir" — never by his first name. Older classmen were looked up to.

"The Jigger Shop was the afternoon eatery and located in the small house down near the Power House at the end of the lower athletic field. A PB&J or hamburger, a Coke or milkshake were the popular items. Clothiers J. Press, Langrock and Rosenbergs would come to campus displaying their wares. Munson Gallery would also come at the beginning of a school year offering the opportunity for students to buy pictures, which they could use to decorate their rooms.

"During the 1940-41 academic year sports events were held with other schools on a pretty normal schedule. This was to change the following year with gasoline rationing. Choate, Deerfield, Hotchkiss and Kent were our principal rivals and games were held with these independent schools plus local high schools. In other words, as the war effort increased, sporting events with other schools were curtailed. We had good healthy rivalry in the club system — Alpha, Beta and Gamma — everyone at Taft being affiliated with one of the clubs. Varsity football and track were held up at Rockefeller Field, all others on the lower fields or in the gym, a part of the main building. Hockey was on natural ice, when we had it, on the pond at the back of the school. Boards, probably 2' high, were assembled. If one gave a body check to another, there was usually a time-out to reassemble the side-boards. After practice, everyone chipped in to scrape and broom-sweep the pond so that it could be sprayed in the evening to form a new surface for the following day. In March, before the Easter vacation and before the spring semester, we had daily exercise of Walk-Run. It was just that — run for a goodly distance and then a short walk. Supposedly, it helped to get in condition for track. It was viewed by all of us as a most unpopular form of exercise.

"The Upper Classmen had one dance each year, usually in the winter term. It was a formal affair and chaperoned by the faculty and wives. The gym was beautifully decorated. Usually there were one or two sports events. At noon Sunday, the girls departed and we were back to a monastic society. Paul Cruikshank was Headmaster and Mr. McIntosh the Dean. Seniors usually had counselling sessions with Paul to determine college choice. Academic and mis-conduct problems were handled by the Dean. . . .

"With the intensity of the war, we saw many of the Faculty and Staff leave school to serve their country. The students took on more and more responsibility in running the school. I remember well returning as a Corridor Monitor in my Senior year to cover the kitchen corridor, there being a shortage of Masters to cover this area. Our class of 1943 implemented the Work Program which is still in force over forty years later. We washed and broomed floors, cleaned classrooms, emptied trash, waited on table, etc. Every-one chipped in. We even went to various local farms, notably Lyman Orchard, to pick fruit. The war effort was at a high pitch and we had to do all sorts of chores to help the school function. Each noon time there was a Work Assembly where those who were delinquent in their chores were brought to the attention of the student body. Such laggards got extra duty in the after-noon raking leaves or moving trash or shoveling snow, whatever needed to be done. So often people have asked me why members of 1943 had such loyalty, esprit de corps, not only when we were at Taft, but for our school in the ensuing years. I attribute it to the responsibilities we took on at the time. . . .

"A fact that I believe to be accurate and of interest is that dur-ing the war years Taft's tuition dropped from $1,450.00 to $1,250.00 per year. Undoubtedly this is the only decrease in the school's history. This occurred because the student body took on so much of the extra work in keeping the school going.

In 1942 the Masque and Dagger presented a memorable performance of "Arsenic & Old Lace" with Horace Taft '43 as Teddy Roosevelt, shown here with his somewhat startled and reserved father, Senator Robert A. Taft '06. Horace later became a distinguished professor of Physics and Dean of the Faculty at Yale, as well as Chairman of Taft's Board of Trustees.

"Due to the war, virtually everyone travelled by public transportation — bus and train. Gas rationing limited travel. We did not go home for Thanksgiving and Easter. Seniors and maybe Upper Mids, as I recall, had only one weekend a semester. Others had none. Thanks to Spyros Skouras we had some first rate movies for Saturday nights. The war was further brought home when Paul Cruikshank announced at Vespers those many alumni who had been killed in action. We, as Seniors, had to face the decision of whether to enlist or go on to college. Because I was 19 at the time, my local Draft Board was after me before I had even graduated. This was the case with many of my classmates. In the two years to follow, word reached me of the deaths of two dear friends — Jud Conant and Jim Palmer. The former was a Marine and killed in the Pacific. How well I remember trailing him on Walk-Run or in track. It would be almost impossible for present day Taft students or faculty to sense how quickly we matured as high school seniors because of the war. It was a memorable and sobering era." ■

The War Years

The years 1941-45 obviously saw many changes at the school. Some of them as seen from the perspective of a student have been related by Henry Estabrook '43. Many of the changes, such as food rationing, obtained only during the years of actual conflict, but some — such as the job program — became a permanent part of the structure of the school.

The enrollment stayed remarkably steady:

296	1942-43
293	1943-44
296	1944-45

and, despite the addition of courses in navigation and artillery, the basic core of the curriculum remained much as it had been in the pre-war years. The Headmaster summed up the attitude of the school in December 1941: "These are days of confusion and anxiety. Never in our time has there been greater uncertainty about the future...(but) we are facing the future with confidence and courage."

It is significant to note that even in the middle of the war years, Mr. Cruikshank was able to take a longer view of the days ahead. In December 1942, he announced a "Program for the Future" — a program that would bring to the school diverse lecturers speaking of world problems and challenges. "The generation now in school must broaden its vision beyond the Atlantic and Pacific coast lines and must be instilled with the idea of service not only to the nation, but to the world." This was a noble concept and, if the program never completely realized its potential, it was surely a step in the direction of breaking the rather insular view many Americans had held in the pre-war years.

The handsome war memorial honoring Taft's 59 World War II dead.

Dean McIntosh

On Alumni Day 1947, Andrew McIntosh retired after 44 years at Taft. Although he eventually became Chairman of the History Department, he is principally known as the School's first Dean, and it was in this capacity that he helped Horace Taft establish the central character of the school. In its June farewell, the Papyrus saluted his retirement: "There can be no doubt as to the prominent part he has played in the school's development... The statistics of his life tell part of the story. But what they cannot say is what he has stood for to generation on generation of Taft students — his kindliness, his understanding, his sense of scholarliness. Nor can these things be said now, but they are deep in the hearts of those who have gone before and those who are here now."

It is interesting to note from a vantage point of 45 years some of the prognostications of the speakers who came to Taft under the program: Dennis McEvoy, Moscow Correspondent for the Columbia Broadcasting System, foresaw a "Europe Red from Gibraltar to Kamchatka," a world in which there would be two capitals — "Washington and Moscow". Right on target. But a later speaker, Sir Girja Bajpai, Minister Plenipotentiary from India to the United States, was looking into a clouded crystal ball when he predicted that unity between the Moslem and Hindu groups was not by any means impossible, but was, in fact, well on the way to realization.

In February 1943 Mr. Taft died, and the outpouring of love and affection for the founder of the school was ample testimony to the tremendous influence this one life had on so many others. Tributes from old boys, faculty, and fellow headmasters filled much of a memorial edition of the *Alumni Bulletin*.

And despite the larger events occurring outside the school, the minutiae of everyday life went on. In the fall of 1942, Mr. Cruikshank decided that the traditional Fall Dance should not be held — to save gasoline and the extra money such affairs inevitably consumed. Naturally enough, this particular sacrifice for the war effort did not hit a responsive chord with the Seniors of that day. The *Papyrus* asked with some asperity, "If it is a question of saving money, why not provide a free weekend for the two upper classes?" This would provide a much-needed break at no cost to the school. The idea was not accepted by "the authorities," and the next *Papyrus* editorial supported the Headmaster's decision. But it is highly significant to note that the school *did,* in fact, have a Winter Dance that year and, yes, even a Spring Dance!

THE TAFT ALUMNI BULLETIN

Volume 20	WATERTOWN, CONNECTICUT, JANUARY, 1945	Number 1

The Headmaster's Page

As I sit at my desk this Sunday afternoon it is snowing hard outside. Already six or eight inches of snow have piled up on the ledge outside my office window. The boys on the hockey squad are out on the pond shoveling, and losing ground to the storm. Mr. Pennell and some of the penalty crew boys for the day are out shoveling the walks to the infirmary and to the Annex. (Most of you do not know of the penalty crew, a group of unfortunates who did their jobs poorly this morning and so have to put in some extra work this afternoon . . . a wartime institution.)

This morning there was a grand sermon at the Church by Dr. Wendell Phillips of Rye, but the singing was rather poor, as it always seems to be the first Sunday after vacation. After Church a group of Seniors gathered at my house for a cup of coffee and a chat with Dr. Phillips, and the discussion, as usual, covered a wide range of human experience.

Many of the boys are out on the golf course, up by the Field House, on skis for the first time this winter. Somewhere over my head on the Upper Middle corridor there's a roughhouse that I ought to go up and stop. The Lower Middle Committee has just been in to see me about the informal tea dance they are having next Saturday with some Westover girls. Some parents with a very frightened-looking little boy are being shown about the school with a view toward the boy's entering Taft next fall. I fear the rooms they see will look as they always look on a Sunday afternoon, and I will have to talk at tomorrow's assembly on neatness.

At tonight's Vespers the Seniors will choose the hymns, and I can almost guess in advance what ones they will choose. We shall close with "Now the Day is Over." After Vespers Mrs. Cruikshank and I are having Seniors in for supper and we'll sit around the fireplace for a while afterwards. Then a meeting with the monitors, and then to bed.

There really is no point to this letter, except that I've been thinking about you, scattered all over the world, in France, in Belgium, in New Guinea, the Philippines, China, Africa. And I thought you'd like to remember a Sunday at Taft. It hasn't changed much.

Paul Cruikshank

1943 saw students working on nearby farms, faculty wives working in war plants, monitors supervising evening study hall, and Lowell Thomas making one of his regular evening broadcasts from the stage of Bingham Auditorium.

1944 witnessed a Mid-year commencement and *three* head-monitors, as each one left successively to join the armed forces.

Throughout the war, Mr. Cruikshank wrote a "Headmaster's Letter" that appeared on Page 1 of the Alumni Bulletin. In many ways, these letters show him at his best, and one of them is reproduced in full on Page 67.

With the end of the war in 1945, the school was able to sum up — with justifiable pride — its contribution to the Allied victory. More than 1,400 Taft alumni — more than half of all alumni living at that time — served in uniform — either in one of the U.S. branches of service or in foreign units. Major Ralph Cheli '37 was awarded the Congressional Medal of Honor posthumously, for heroic service in the South Pacific. In all, Taft lost 59 men who died in service.

The Post-War Years

The school — like the nation — recovered quickly from the war. The energy and confidence that seemed to flow endlessly during the war years was channeled in new directions. In the August 1946 Bulletin, the Headmaster was able to say: "Applications for admission in the fall have topped by a wide margin all previous records, and the result is that we look forward to having an outstanding student body.... We have gone through the first confusing year of the post-war period with a scholastic record of which we can be proud; we are in a sound financial condition; we have a strong and loyal faculty....I look forward with enthusiasm and confidence."

To show just how "normal" things were back in the late forties, it may be instructive to reproduce a part of a *Papyrus* editorial from November 1948. The school had just experienced a disastrous Fall sports schedule, and the lead editorial of the November 20th issue reminded the student "That preparation for college and life thereafter is the real goal and must be kept in mind by those who wish to maintain an objective sense of balance and proportion in viewing school athletics."

Charles Beane Weld, known to everyone as "Beanie", was in many ways the quintessential schoolmaster. For 39 years his dry Yankee wit enlivened Taft classrooms as he labored to expand the literary horizons of his students and at the same time to teach them the glories of an honest English sentence. His tenure — 1911 to 1950 — spanned a period of extraordinary growth at Taft both in buildings and curriculum. After he left Taft, he taught at day schools in Florida and California, and at one time made a memorable appearance on the Groucho Marx Show.

1950: The Mays Rink, named in honor of Eddie Mays '27, was the first artificial ice hockey rink in prep school circles. Math teacher Len Sargent was the driving spirit behind the building of the rink, which was largely a "do-it-yourself" project with boys and faculty contributing more than 3,000 hours of labor. The addition of the roof in 1957 made the skating surface truly usable from mid-October to mid-March.

But the second editorial perhaps expressed more succinctly the real mood of the school in the dark days of the Fall term:

"These are the days that try men's souls, requiring the utmost fortitude from all. Tucked away in Watertown as we have been for eight weeks, Christmas vacation still seems far distant. Football is over, and the Winter sports have not begun. Adding no small degree of shading to the grey gloom hovering over the school, the all-important quarterly exams have just been finished. Life, we add portentously, is a grim business.

"Accordingly, we decided to dig deep into our psyche for some of the 'gripes' which are rife in all of us at such a time. We are doing so in order that, by getting them off our chest, we may better continue on our way, unburdened by any hidden complexes. Thus, fiercely we demand why the Administration doesn't:

1. Cease giving serious soaks for cutting meals, especially breakfast, since the hungry feeling seems punishment enough.

2. Allow class cuts on Saturday to students who maintain a seventy-five average in that subject.

3. Require the kitchen to serve corn flakes whenever bananas comprise the fruit for breakfast.

4. See that the mail is out by the end of the first period.

5. Investigate the reason for Mr. Fenton's reluctance to talk in Vespers.

6. Set up a recreation room in the basement with ping-pong and pool tables and a bowling alley.

7. Return to the penalty crew system, whereby one could improve his citizenship rating by working off certain soaks.

8. Allow the school the Wednesday-to-Sunday Thanksgiving holiday, which is the rule rather than the exception at other schools.

9. Give the poor waiters back their second tray to ease their job and speed the time between the courses.

10. Return to the four quarters as the basis for earning weekends.

The Cruikshank Faculty

"Moral and scholastic standards, a sound curriculum, a tradition of hard work, an atmosphere of friendliness — all of these and more, too, are important if a school is to succeed in giving the finest possible educational experience to its boys. All these attributes become meaningless, though — or perhaps even cease to exist — unless those who are responsible in the school for the instruction and guidance of its students are persons of worth and stature. Teaching techniques, academic qualifications, enthusiasm — these are not enough. Still most vital in a school is the stature of the 'man on the other end of the log'."

— Paul Cruikshank, 1953

In Mr. Cruikshank's first year as Headmaster, the faculty consisted of 28 men, 12 of whom had advanced degrees. With a student body of 331, the teacher/pupil ratio was approximately 12:1. In his last year, there were 46 men and 365 students, for a teacher/pupil ratio of 8:1. It is interesting to note that the number of advanced degrees in 1962 (21) stayed in about the same proportion as 1936 — that is, about half the faculty had some kind of degree beyond the bachelor's. But the drop in the teacher/pupil ratio is remarkable.

Of the 46 faculty in 1962, 8 were appointees of Horace Taft. And five of the eight held key administrative responsibilities.

Joe Cunningham was one of the first men hired by Mr. Cruikshank and through the years became probably closer to him than any other faculty member. Although a fine teacher of French, Joe became increasingly involved with administration, finally moving out of the classroom altogether. Serving first as Chairman of the Modern Language Department, Joe successively became Assistant to the Headmaster, Dean, Director of Admissions, and finally Assistant Headmaster. Joe's native intelligence, quick wit, and verbal dexterity contributed to his success, but all of these factors converged into an extraordinary ability to get along well with all sorts of people: he was — and is — a master of human relations.

A student tradition: touching Lincoln's nose to ensure good luck on examinations. Peter Taft '53, son of Charles Phelps Taft '13, keeps the tradition alive.

Joe's insights into the Cruikshank method of dealing with his faculty are uniquely valuable, and he was finally prevailed upon (in 1985) to put them on paper:

Some Musings and Observations Prompted By the Faculty Photo of 1960

By Joseph I. Cunningham

The 1960 faculty

During any given year in the decade from 1952 until 1962, as I talked about Taft with interested students and their parents (and I only did at first, of course, if the Headmaster was busy!), I could usually assure them with pride that our faculty was relatively young, truly competent, of remarkable depth and equalled by very few in New England and, moreover, that they worked extremely hard, enjoyed their work and the young people with whom they lived and, usually (!) each other.

Many of Mr. Cruikshank's appointees stayed the course, to be sure. Some didn't work out and others, full of ability and ambition and sometimes probably a bit frustrated by the presence of our entrenched new old guard, went on to other careers. In the education field they included several pre-school department chairmen, a number of college professors, one college president, and thirteen secondary school headmasters from Connecticut and New York to Ohio, Oklahoma, Texas and California.

One might think that a man who took over Taft in the middle of the Depression, found it to have a sizable debt instead of an endowment like its competitors, and within a couple of years was assailed by the upheaval and confusion of World War II and managed to bring the School safely through it all would feel, upon retirement most proud of that achievement. Not so of Mr. C. He was proudest of and felt a great indebtedness to all of those "good men" of his who had contributed to the growth and development of the boys, and through them, to Taft, the School.

For most of his time at Taft he did not have the financial resources to hire (appoint!) many men with much experience. He had to depend on his judgment and acumen to find "good men" who, though largely untried, seemed to deserve the chance to develop in our community. When the school was smaller and without admissions apparatus, he chose "good boys" the same way if

he could find them. Naturally he didn't get a hit every time but he didn't strike out often either.

Like every headmaster he started out with a specific need or job to be filled and he interviewed men whose resumes indicated they had the necessary educational background or talent. Beyond that he dug and dug seeking intuitively for signs of potential for growth as a person in the life at Taft. Once we were faculty members, only rarely did he get directly involved in everything else! He might very well call us in to talk about lapses in attendance, promptness, discipline, dress, personal habits and eccentricities and judgment. He never ceased to be rather surprised and disappointed when some men got upset, hurt, angry, defensive or made excuses because they thought perhaps that he was treating them like the students, or worse. He, in turn, clearly thought that he was treating each of them as a man, one who had the same goal as he did — to be the best Taft School master he could be — and

In May 1955 Headmaster Cruikshank was invited by the Secretary of Defense to participate in a Joint Civilian Orientation Conference to demonstrate the country's military program then in place. The group of 80 men from all over the country visited several military installations, including two days at sea aboard the aircraft carrier Intrepid, and two days at Eglin Field, Florida, where the Headmaster was taken on a jet fight aboard an Air Force T-33.

Harlin A. Sexton — "Sox" to one and all — came to Taft in 1919 to teach Math, but is probably best remembered as one of the first teachers of what was then known as "Remedial English." With his wife Ora, "Sox" developed a pioneering program in this field during the 1940s. A 1911 graduate of Harvard, the 6′3″ Sexton was a star pitcher on its varsity baseball team, snapped Yale's eleven-year home game winning streak, and was elected to the All-Eastern team. In 1946 he gave what director Robert Olmstead called a "shining performance" as the Stage Manager in a memorable faculty-student production of Thornton Wilder's "Our Town." He retired in 1954.

maybe a little better. If this approach was as destructive of initiative, self-confidence and innovation as some few felt, I can't help but wonder how it happened that so very, very many inexperienced young men turned out to be very dynamic, creative, confident, individualistic, gung-ho colleagues.

Now Mr. Cruikshank didn't share these men's knowledge as such but *they* shared *his* view of teaching as, without being preachy or doctrinaire, a moral endeavor, and they carried out their responsibilities accordingly. As he had hoped and believed they would, they became schoolmasters, not mere purveyors of "expertise."

The sociologists of the '60s told us our lives, students' and teachers' alike, were dull, sterile and lacking in meaning and purpose for "the real world". Not many of us remember it that way. ∎

Arthur Thomas

Arthur Thomas, whose teaching of Latin extended even to the schoolboy Latinizing of his name — "Tomae" — was one of a group of five Middlebury men on the faculty between the wars. (The others: C.B. Weld, Duane Robinson, George Wilson, Howard Farwell. Only Yale, with eight, had more representatives on the 32-man faculty in 1940.) The quintessential thrifty, laconic Vermonter, Thomas once told a young colleague: "I find I use a box of chalk every ten years." Notorious for his strict classroom demeanor, Thomas struck terror into the hearts of his young charges, but also embedded the Latin. His Vespers were always looked forward to by the students, not because of their uplifting message, but because of their brevity. Invariably he simply strode to the podium, read the 23rd Psalm, and walked out.

Alumni of the 1950s will recall Mr. Cruikshank's running feud with Winston cigarettes about the use of the preposition "like" in their ad: "Winston tastes good — like a cigarette should." The Winston president replied (in a letter the Headmaster read in Vespers), "I agree with you, but I can't fight the advertising men." (To which Mr. Cruikshank replied with a more genteel equivalent of "baloney.") In any event, the company did make at least a moderate gesture in the direction of good grammar as evidenced by the advertisement placed in the Columbia University Humor magazine, the *Jester.* Bob Fry '57 sent the revised ad to the Headmaster with a comment that "Winston was making an exception, not setting a precedent."

Continuing a Taft headmaster tradition: meeting with the monitors. Here Paul Cruikshank confers with the 1950 Senior monitors.

Alumni Day 1955: Charlie and Jeanne Shons receive the traditional silver bowl from Alumni Association President Seymour Dribben '27 at their retirement. Charlie came to Taft in 1922 as an Instructor in French, but is most remembered as Director of Athletics. A colorful figure with a fine tenor voice, Charlie participated in many dramatic productions both at the school and in summer stock in Litchfield, Waterbury, and Southbury. He was a member of Actors Equity. As Athletic Director, Charlie organized the intramural club system (Alpha, Beta, Gamma) as well as introducing the sport of soccer to the school. His athletic notices on the bulletin board were part of school legend. For example: "GOXers and SISHEG take long walk to swale beyond red barn." Translation: "General outdoor Exercisers and Special Ineligible Study Hall Exercise Group take a walk to a certain point in the country." He served in France during World War I in the Field Artillery and was known henceforth as "Major", until he returned to active duty in WW II, after which he was known as "Colonel". Jeanne Shons was for many years the School Librarian and also served as Librarian of the Watertown Library. A handsome and gregarious couple, the Shonses epitomized the ideal boarding school family, taking obvious delight in every aspect of their life at Taft and achieving the difficult task of being popular with both faculty and students.

Waiting on Table

The system of students waiting on table was a short-lived phenomenom. For the first fifty years of the school, maids waited on table. Not until World War II did the Job Program come into existence, as vividly related by Henry Estabrook '43. And by 1959 — 16 years later — the construction of the Armstrong Dining Hall made it possible for waiters to sit at the table they were serving and eat their meal at the same time, albeit a bit hurriedly. "Waiting on Table" was still a part of the job program, but it was considerably scaled down: no more white jackets, no more waiters' meal.

Waiting was without doubt the most difficult task of the Job Program. Each boy could expect a two week tour of duty twice a year. It was a grueling two weeks, adding about an hour a day to an already crowded schedule. In addition, it was usually the source of a goodly number of "soaks" — or demerits — on a student's disciplinary record. The waiting routine was carefully, even rigidly, organized and supervised. The command system was composed of three headwaiters who served throughout the year. Thus they were the supreme authorities on procedure, and the source of most of the "soaks" for unsatisfactory waiting. In addition to the three headwaiters, two faculty members were also pressed into service. This task was assigned only to the most junior faculty, some of whom were experiencing fledgling difficulties with discipline and to whom the Dining Room Duty offered simply more exposure to enemy fire, that is to say, to frustrated, angry, rebellious — and experienced — students.

The waiters were expected to arrive at the kitchen at least five minutes before

One of the most grueling jobs in the system — waiting on table. Mr. Fenton and Mr. Farwell serve.

(another Steve Sherer original)

75

Steve Sherer's '57 bewildered new boy arriving in the main circle.

the serving hour; they "checked in" with one of the headwaiters, donned their white jackets, and each secured a large tray. Then they lined up just outside the swinging doors (photo above), in order of the number of the table they were assigned to for the two-week period. Ferociously silenced by the headwaiter during the saying of grace in the main dining hall, they emerged at the end of the prayer serially, for all the world like a chorus line kicking its way on stage out of the wings. At times, the rebellious troops would produce a rhythmic clanging sound by banging their trays against their knees as they marched down the aisle. Taking their position behind the master's chair and alongside the waiter's table, they were expected to remain silent, but at immediate call by the table master. There was no "slumping" — no leaning on the table — and headwaiters and masters patrolled the ranks to enforce the rule. The waiters had been

trained in the etiquette of serving, including such niceties as "crumbing" the table after the main course but before dessert was served. Depending on the strictness of the master, this was a custom more frequently honored in the breach than in the observance.

No discussion of the rigors and perils of waiting on table would be complete without recounting one of the most legendary incidents in the waiting saga. At one routine dinner in the middle of the winter term, a tired, careless waiter moving too fast, upturned an entire serving bowl of mashed turnip over the head of senior faculty member Dan Fenton. The clangor of the metal dish hitting the floor and the gasp of dismay at Mr. Fenton's table immediately

THE PRESIDENT RECEIVES THE AMBASSADOR TO MEXICO
AND HIS FAMILY — see pages 10 and 11.
World Wide-Photos, Inc.

A 1957 Alumni Bulletin article commented on the number of Taft men then active in government service. Bob Hill '38 and his family are shown here on the cover with President Eisenhower at the time of his appointment as Ambassador to Mexico. He had previously been Ambassador to El Salvador and later served as Ambassador to Spain. Also pictured in the Bulletin article were Harold Tittman '12, Ambassador to Haiti and Peru; William Howard Taft III, '33 Ambassador to Ireland; Charles Finucane '24, Undersecretary of the Army; Robert Wagner '29, Mayor of New York City; and Senator Robert Taft '06.

attracted the attention of the entire dining hall. It was a moment of stupendous, awe-struck silence. Mr. Fenton, a man of enormous dignity, arose from the table, disdained to wipe the orangey mess from his brow, and strode out of the hushed dining room. The confused babble of suppressed laughter and caustic comments ("Chase will never get into Yale now" — Fenton was College Admissions Officer) soon replaced the silence. Mr. Fenton suffered slight but painful burns on his face and did not appear on the corridor for two or three days.

Chase did not get into Yale, but he did get into Harvard, and 30 years later sent his one daughter and two sons to Taft. Of such stuff are legends made.

Finally, by the mid-70s, waiting on table was phased out altogether. Students "volunteered" at each table, taking turns to fetch the various courses throughout the meal. And by the 1980s, there were only three "sit-down" meals a week, with students assigned to certain tables. Cafeteria-style dining had become the order of the day.

Henry and Marion Pennell, pictured here at a Hartford dinner with John Learned '20, were a popular faculty couple during the 40s and 50s. Henry, a math teacher and coach of varsity football and baseball, was known as "the Jap" for his sneak attack Math quizzes just as the bell rang ending class. He left Taft to pursue administrative challenges at other independent schools.

Cruikshank Anecdotes

All successful headmasters have an aura about them. With some, it may be one of warmth, understanding, patience, tolerance. For Paul Cruikshank it was *respect*. Many of the 3,000 boys who were at school with him would, perhaps, have termed him cold, or stern, or unbending. Perhaps some actively disliked him. But it is very doubtful if even one of the 3,000 would say he did not thoroughly respect Headmaster Paul Cruikshank. When King Lear asks the Duke of Kent (disguised as a servant) why he wishes to serve him, Kent replies: "Because you have that in your countenance that I would fain call master." "What's that?" the King asks. Kent's one word response, "Authority" has the ring of truth and great conviction behind it. Mr. Cruikshank, too, had the aura of "authority" and "respect" streaming from him. It could be seen in many ways.

Saturday night movies could frequently become boisterous — especially if the film involved even the smallest evidence of sex. The catcalls, sniggers, and off-color remarks would gradually increase as the film went on — despite courageous attempts by monitors to hush 'em up. Suddenly, people would be aware that a tall figure was striding down the aisle to the front of the theatre. Sometimes he needed to say nothing. Other times he might say in a calm, controlled voice: "If there is any more of this sort of behavior, I will close the film down at once." Utter silence. And for the rest of the film decorum prevailed.

And in Vespers — particularly toward the end of Winter Term when spirits flagged and the winter of discontent was obvious on every side — the students would be restless in their seats; undertones of whisperings were rampant. But the Headmaster was at the podium. Suddenly, in the middle of his remarks, he would come full stop: "Saunders, sit up!" The whole auditorium immediately shifted from a spinal sag posture to an erect bearing worthy of West Point. And for the next two weeks (the remark

On Alumni Day 1958, a new and much needed faculty residence was dedicated to honor Dr. Henry Merriman '97, a loyal and devoted alumnus. The Merriman family was one of the many Watertown families who provided encouragement and support for Horace Taft after the school was established in Watertown. Ed and Jean Douglas (on the right behind their dog) were the first faculty occupants of Merriman House. Trustee Donald Buttenheim '33, on the far right, was the principal speaker at the ceremony.

79

Kate Mailliard had a very special and close association with Taft. The widow of J. W. Mailliard, Jr. '09, Mrs. Mailliard had two sons attend the School, William '35 and James '42, as well as three grandsons, William, Jr. '60, Ward '65, and Lawrence '71. In 1959 in memory of her husband, Mrs. Mailliard established the Mailliard Fellowship, intended to recognize excellence in teaching either in or out of the classroom. Since 1967 the Fellowship has been awarded to new college graduates who have joined the faculty as apprentice teachers.

was usually timed to make the effect last until vacation) order again prevailed during the Vespers service.

* * * * * *

One very hot September evening, a new young master was taking his first evening study hall. At the beginning of the study period, one of the seniors asked if the students could take off their jackets. Believing this to be a reasonable request in view of the extreme humidity, the young master agreed, and all of the students promptly removed their jackets, draping them over the back of the chairs. They then got down to work. The study hall had been in progress no more than ten or fifteen minutes when the door opened, and the Headmaster walked in. After a quick glance around the hall, he strode up to the master's desk. "Did you say they could remove their jackets?"

"Yes, sir," replied the nervous young man.

"Well, don't," the headmaster said, and walked out.

* * * * * *

A long-standing Christmas tradition of the Cruikshanks' — lining the bookcases of their living room with the hundreds of Christmas cards they received from their old boys.

A new varsity football coach was called into the Headmaster's office the morning of an important football game — an away game at Loomis. The entire interview, which lasted nearly half an hour, was devoted to the conduct of the team: their manners while traveling on the bus, their behavior on the sidelines, their manners at the tea after the game (be sure that each boy goes up to the lady pouring tea and thanks her before departing) and the like. Not one word was said about hopes for a team victory.

* * * * * *

The same young coach remembers a baseball game a year or so later. The score was tied in the tenth inning; for various reasons, it had been a slow game. The Headmaster walked down to the bench, leaned over to get the coach's ear: "Be sure that the team is inside — properly dressed — in time for 5:15 study hall."

* * * * * *

The Armstrong Dining Room — built in 1959.

Livingston Carroll

Before his untimely death in 1959, Livingston "Pat" Carroll was well on the way to establishing another legend as an outstanding schoolmaster. A 1937 Taft alumnus, Pat had had a fine record as a student: Monitor, Cum Laude, Captain of wrestling and golf, and varsity letterman in soccer. After graduating from Yale in 1941, he returned to Taft to teach for a year before entering military service in WW II. A forward artillery spotter in the European Theater of Operations, Pat was severely wounded and spent a year in hospital before being discharged in 1945 with a Silver Star and Purple Heart. He returned to Taft in 1946 and resumed his career as a teacher of Latin and an outstanding coach of soccer, wrestling, and golf. His sudden death from a heart attack just before the opening of the Fall Term shocked the School community.

81

The 70th Anniversary Development Program held its kick-off dinner at the Waldorf-Astoria, New York City, October 11, 1960. Above are some of the men at the Speakers Table: L. to R., Phelps Platt '36, Del Ladd '44, the Headmaster, Ted Chapin '27, Bob Sweet '40, Sterling Rockefeller '24, and Seymour Dribben '27.

A young master in his first year at the school seemed to be making an excellent start. He had breathed new life into a semi-moribund extra-curricular activity, was popular with the boys, and all in all seemed to be settling in well. There was one small cloud: he had a slight but noticeable speech impediment — a hesitancy, a sort of stutter. One morning after he had been at school a month or so, he was called in to the Headmaster's office. After a few preliminary comments and expressions of satisfaction with the work done thus far, the Headmaster concluded the interview by saying: "You realize, I'm sure, that your stutter sometimes provides a chance for ridicule — for mimicry. You must stop stuttering." The astonished young master stumbled out of the office to the comforting presence of Assistant Headmaster Joe Cunningham, a refuge for dispirited students and faculty alike. Boiling over with indignation, the master poured out his wrath at the seeming heartlessness of the Headmaster. Joe listened quietly until the steam had subsided. "What you say may all be true, Frank, but do you realize you haven't stuttered since you walked into my office?" And legend has it that he never stuttered again.

* * * * * *

J. Irwin Miller '27 was the principal speaker. In his far-sighted remarks he was critical of some of the then current thinking about the mission of the school and of American society in general. "It seems to me that there is nothing more degrading about our society today than our dismal *pre-occupation with survival.*" Rather, Mr. Miller went on, "Even the brightest of us never uses more than a fifth of his potential. . . I will never forget the first time I rowed in a crew race. How frightened I was to find myself completely exhausted — with only one third of the race gone — how elated when I first discovered second wind — this exciting new capacity which I had never known I had.

"Here then is a *special purpose for Taft* — to lead intelligent, sensitive, gifted young men — at the most impressionable time of life — *to discover that second wind of the mind and spirit whose use and exploitation is justification for life itself.*" (all original italics)

Significances — and Trivia — at Mid-Century

This sketch was first used in the fund-raising brochure "Into the Sixties" in 1960. Drawn by Alumni Secretary Dick Lovelace, it served as an unofficial "logo" for many years, appearing in many varieties of Taft printed matter, and even on the back of the Taft chairs.

In retrospect it seems apparent that the fifties were much like any other period in the life of the school — there were high points and there were low points. The dread disease of polio could and did still strike. In October 1948, Jim Johnson was indeed stricken. He eventually recovered and returned to the school to graduate in 1951. In April 1951, the school underwent instruction in atom bomb defense: bomb shelters were prepared in the basement and evacuation drills were practiced. By 1954 the school was convinced that the "Indo-China War" was a very important issue, and a

L. to R. Peggy Lovelace, Betty Cunningham, Joyce Poole ('74!), Lee Poole, Marge Currie, Shirley Clark.

Faculty Wives

From the very beginning, faculty wives have been an integral part of school life. It was not a role suitable for just any woman, for living on a corridor with sixty active teenagers, eating dinner at a table for twelve, rearing one's own children in an environment only partially under one's immediate control — all of these factors could make for difficulties. Still, there were compensations: the feeling of being an important part of the husband's life and the belief that they did, indeed, contribute a measure of warmth and color to what otherwise might have been a rather monastic environment. They poured at teas, chaperoned dances, and opened their homes to returning alumni and other "guests of the school." At times they were even pressed into service "above and beyond." Pictured is a group of volunteers getting out a mailing at the height of the Development Program in the sixties. And Marietta Sullivan is shown presiding at a typical tea table.

Mr. Cruikshank and Sterling Rockefeller '24 cut the ribbon to open the 70th Anniversary Science Center.

poll of the student body turned up the interesting information that a majority favored compulsory military training.

In the fall of 1952 the school acquired two TV sets which were placed in the Upper School and Middle Common Rooms. In 1954 these sets made it possible for the school to watch one of the most fascinating political dramas of the decade: the Senatorial hearings of Senator Joseph McCarthy.

But to show that the more things change the more they remain the same, it should be pointed out that politically, the students were as far off as ever: in the 1948 student polls Dewey defeated Truman by a large majority. The presence of some master satirists in the 1953-54 student body made it possible to publish another issue of the Taft "Perspyrus" and to produce a vastly successful musical entitled "The Queen and I" — largely a spoof of the masters.

But the ugly face of progress was being seen: In 1952 a major hurdle was overcome when it was announced that loafers were no longer illegal — a decision that would have gladdened the hearts of the 1943 editors who claimed (as part of the war effort) that during the war "we must learn to make use of what we have. ...There are 200 pair of illegal shoes in the school. Why not use them?" The Headmaster's response to this plea was that the school would soon take on "a sloppy appearance," and that the privilege would be abused. Like mothers, Headmasters are frequently right, as the *Papyrus* had to admit in 1955 when somewhat apologetically they made a plea for khakis as proper wear for class. "Students have abused the privilege of wearing loafers... and consequently are

Dedication of the 70th Anniversary Science Center, November 5, 1961, brought out an impressive assemblage of Taft notables. The construction of this building represented the first step in a major architectural decision: to turn the school's back on Route 6 and shift the center of the school from the front (main) circle to the Pond area in the rear of the school. Pictured here are three of the many generous Taft families who helped bring about this fine addition to the school: The Klingensteins (at top), the Snyders (center) and the Stotts (at bottom).

in a vulnerable position." But with the eternal optimism of youth they decreed that khakis would be different; students "would make an effort to keep their khakis clean."

It was also in 1952 that the school undertook to provide a modest form of sex education. The program consisted chiefly of individual counselling — mostly from the Headmaster — but the Library made available a collection of books and pamphlets that were easily accessible to the students on open shelves and with no need to "sign out." The Alumni Bulletin published a list of the books for the information of alumni who "may face the problem of sex education with their own children."

Despite the fact that the fifties were generally regarded as rather "quiescent" with some masters complaining that students didn't rebel *enough,* a careful observer might have noted early warning of the tumultuous sixties in the move away from contact sports to "less rigorous" games. That Fall, soccer had greatly increased in popularity; during the winter increasing numbers of boys opted for "G.O.X." (general outdoor exercise) rather than the traditional sports of hockey and basketball; in the spring baseball and track were again "pressed for numbers." The *Papyrus* urged that "boys in their teens should not allow themselves to become weak . . . . we should reconsider our attitude toward exercise, for the 'contact sports' do offer a physical challenge — a goal toward which a boy may strive."

In short, as one looks back over the 1950s — especially the latter part of the decade — one is struck by the mixture of the traditional idyllic life of boarding school within its ivied walls and the increasing intrusiveness of the outside world. For example, in May 1956, Steve Sherer — one of Taft's most gifted cartoonists — proved that he was as versa-

tile in prose as with pen and ink by writing a humorous plea for the "gramophone privilege" — a privilege once enjoyed during the roaring twenties, and banned at that time by Chaplain Arthur Howe, who denounced its "degenerating effect."

In the fall of 1957, Louis Martinez, disdaining a declared holiday, opted instead to bicycle six miles to Woodbury, where he succeeded in talking himself into a short but cordial interview with Marilyn Monroe, married at that time to playwright Arthur Miller.

Another minor sociological footnote for future editions of "Preppie" Handbooks: of the 86 girls attending the 1956 Spring Dance, there were 6 Lindas, 4 Sandys, 2 Sandras, 2 Judys, and one each Dodie, Jackie, Freddie, Sherry, Franny, Penny, Ginnie, Winnie.

New York alumni dinners are always popular: this one at the Union Club in March 1961, shows the Executive Committee of the Alumni Association at their meeting prior to the dinner, and below, Bernhard Auer '35 and Orin Lehman '38 during the cocktail hour.

Early Warnings of the Turbulent Sixties

A view of the Pond area showing the new buildings that changed the center of gravity of the school from Woodbury Road (Route 6) to the back of the school. At left is Congdon House, built in 1927 to house the Service Staff, renovated in 1963 for use as a boys dormitory. In 1971 it was again renovated to accommodate the arrival of girls. In the center is the Hulbert Taft, Jr. Library (1969) and at right is the 70th Anniversary Science Center (1961).

But the grim realities of the world *were* beginning to intrude. The launching of Sputnik in 1957 shook the West out of its complacent post-war attitude. At Taft, the school welcomed a refugee from the ill-fated Hungarian revolt. And already some of the catch-phrases of the 1960s were being heard. A 1958 *Papyrus* editorial discussed the problem of conformity, defending it with a quotation from William H. Whyte, Jr.: "...rebellion against opinion merely because it is prevailing should no more be praised than acquiescence to it." "Be yourself," the *Pap* concluded. "Our present age of the Sputniks and the increased emphasis on science is more conducive to individuality of thought than any time in the past two decades. We can aid our country and ourselves by being the individual each of us was intended to be."

In June of the same year an anonymous letter to the *Papyrus* attempted "to clarify the meaning of a previously undefined phrase — *negative attitude*. The term applies to anyone who purposely flaunts the administration, who violates the school's regulations merely for the sake of violating them." Although the writer attempted to

87

The helicopter age arrives for busy men, such as Mason Gross '29, who flew up for a trustees meeting, Spring 1963. Pictured here as he boarded the copter for his return to his duties as President of Rutgers University: son Charlie Gross '64, Mr. Gross, Headmaster Cruikshank, Henry "Ted" Luria '28, Charles Finucane '24, Sterling Rockefeller '24, and Edith Cruikshank.

put a positive spin on the phrase (the Administration should not label as "negative" and treat as a "serious offense" every petty misdemeanor) the phrase did, in fact, come into widespread use during the next few years — even being abbreviated to "N.A."

The drumbeat of rebellion was rumbling in the distance. In April 1959 Upper Middlers made an unsuccessful plea for unlimited late lights. A year and a half later one of the first of many editorials inveighing against "pressure" appeared: "The world is asking too much of its students these days." An "attitude of indifference" was noted in May 1961; that same month another *Papyrus* editorial bewailed the growth of cynicism and of "anarchists who glibly advocate elimination of all save the most basic school rules."..The school needs "mature cooperation for which one can vainly search in this year's school."

The voices became increasingly strident. A November 1961 editorial complained about strict punishment for cutting exercise. The student must have "opportunity to become independent and to think for himself...the school's rules and regulations hinder our actions...we may expect to be stripped of our rights as students to think and act freely."

It is true that moderate voices were still being raised — the '60s were just beginning. In October 1961 *Papyrus* editor Tim Mayer questioned whether age 14-18 is an "auspicious time to commence rebellion from a pattern."

And in 1962 Editor Charlie Hull produced a thoughtful editorial on the subject of individual responsibility. "Modern man is attempting some sort of emancipation of the spirit, which he hopes might bring about a spiritual fulfillment. He feels that he can effect this emancipation only through a state of being which he calls 'free'.

"This logic is hardly more than a subterfuge...a misconception of freedom. The past decade has witnessed sundry displays of individualism as manifested in beatnikism and other such non-conformist movements. Non-conformity, though a freedom not insidious in itself, may take such a firm grasp on the fervent adherent that he loses all regard and consideration for his fellow man."

Mr. Cruikshank Retires

Paul Cruikshank had long maintained that he would retire at 65 — even though he was under no obligation to do so — as were the regular faculty members at that time. But years ago he had observed Headmasters who had stayed on beyond their time when (his words) "they were no longer effective in their role." Some of Mr. Cruikshank's thinking at this time is illuminating. Part of his belief that he should retire seems to have been prompted by matters of immediate concern, while other factors were more deep-rooted, philosophical convictions.

The first instance concerned some of the aberrations of the student upheaval of the 1960s — specifically long hair. "This fad — that is what I fervently hope and pray it will prove to be — of long hair would have so distressed and irked me that I fear I might have become irrational about it and would have let it assume an unmerited and unjustifiable importance. I don't doubt that, in my determination and efforts to eliminate the practice, I may well have neglected matters which were far, far more important to the School's quality and well-being."

The second factor in his determination to retire was more deep-seated and fundamental. "One of the most cogent (reasons for retirement) is that, after many years of experience and service, he is, understandably, inclined to become inflexible in his thinking and attitudes and to have too much confidence in the wisdom he has acquired. Since youth keeps constantly changing, an open mind, a flexible point of view, a fresh look and genuine resiliency are needed by the school administrator, if he is going to provide sound and effective

A happy moment at the Cruikshanks' retirement dinner: the Plaza Hotel, New York City, April 19, 1963. With the Headmaster are L. to R., Robert Taft '35, Robert Sweet '40, Mason Gross '29.

leadership for his institution. It is a safe rule of thumb, I am persuaded, that once each generation the reins of responsibility should be handed over to a much younger man."

In any event, these two streams of thought converged in the spring of 1962, and the search for his successor was under way. *Time* magazine noted the occasion in an interview which quoted Mr. Cruikshank as saying that after retirement, he would "open a small gas station in a remote part of Idaho." This jocular, off-hand remark elicited several responses, some humorous and some serious; one proprietor of such a gasoline station offered his property for sale. The

Headmaster deftly and courteously answered all of the many letters with appropriate demurrers.

The "big event" of the retirement was a gala dinner in New York City at the ballroom of the Plaza Hotel. Nearly seven hundred alumni, parents, friends, and Cruikshank family members assembled to honor Mr. and Mrs. Cruikshank. Trustee Bob Sweet '40 was the toastmaster, and managed the various speakers with grace and aplomb except for Lowell Thomas, who insisted on shutting off the air conditioning while he trekked interminably up the Himalayas.

Earlier in the year at Alumni Day, the Alumni Citation of Merit was presented jointly to Mr. and Mrs. Cruikshank: "Your steadfast belief in your cause enabled you to overcome the trouble presented by great depressions, world conflicts, and the ingenious guerilla war conducted by the spirited youth committed to your charge."

Edith Cruikshank Honored by Taft Mothers

The contribution that Edith Cruikshank made to the school cannot be overestimated. Above she is shown greeing the girls arriving for Dance Weekend; below is the elaborate charm bracelet presented to her by a delegation of mothers at the time of the Cruikshank retirement in 1963.

On Mother's Day, 1963, Mrs. Cruikshank was presented with a unique charm bracelet depicting the facets of her life at Taft. The items on the charm reflected the appreciation of the mothers and parents for all of Edith Cruikshank's contributions to the well-being of the school over the 27 years. It is worth mentioning some of the silver items: "a school bell, a typical Upper Middler with his trousers inches above his shoe tops, a carpet bag for the 28,368 miles you have traveled for the Development Campaign, flowers which you are constantly arranging and forcing, a bed for the thousands of parents and girls whom you put up overnight, a dancing couple for the 75 Formal Dance Weekends involving 8,100 girls (each of whom received your personal note, inviting her to be a guest at Taft), a coffee pot for the 10,304 cups of coffee consumed by Mothers at these weekends over the part fourteen years, a cup and saucer for the unlimited amount of cocoa consumed by boys," etc.

At last it was over, the Cruikshanks *did* take the trip to Greece offered by the Alumni Association, and then left Connecticut for Mr. Esty's first academic year just as Mr. Taft had done for Mr. Cruikshank 27 years earlier. On their return, they purchased a small house in nearby Middlebury, where they lived for many years until failing health necessitated a move to a retirement home. Mr. Cruikshank died December 4, 1985.

Drama Highlights

The crew of the Reluctant
gathers to explore the
Regulations in *Mister Roberts*,
1956.

A noteworthy production of
Billy Budd in 1953 starred
James Franciscus '53.
Franciscus went on to a
Hollywood and T.V. career.

John T. Reardon

John T. Reardon was regarded by many as Taft's finest teacher. Known to the boys as "Jocko", Jack Reardon brought Modern European History to life for generations of Taft students, his distinctive nasal twang and his Socratic approach to classroom discussion insuring that no boy ever fell asleep in his class. To stimulate debate, he often took the unpopular side of a topic and with deft questions, forced his students to think through the opposing argument. A simple but effective teaching technique, writing the "vocabulary word of the week" on the blackboard, helped enlarge the vocabulary of his students immensely during the course of the year. Always immaculately dressed, he was frequently voted "handsomest faculty member" in Senior polls. A 1914 graduate of Dartmouth, where he was president of Phi Beta Kappa and valedictorian of his class, he was awarded the Tuck Fellowship for foreign study, which he spent at the American Academy in Rome, where he received his Master's degree. An instinctive

competitor, he parlayed modest athletic skills into top flight performances. As a boy at Boston Latin School, he played baseball with Joe Kennedy, and later played tennis with Bill Tilden. His favorite milieu, however, was the golf course, where his indifference to pressure and his tongue-in-cheek one upsmanship frequently devastated better players. He served for many years as President of the Watertown Golf Club. A lifelong Democrat in a school almost entirely populated with Republicans and sons of Republicans, he stood for election as State Senator three times. He spent his energy generously outside the School, serving as examiner for the College Entrance Examination Board, a founder of the Connecticut History Teachers Association, and as a member of the Watertown Board of Education and Town Council. After his retirement in 1954 Jack and his wife Louise (for several years secretary to Horace Taft himself) lived on Nova Scotia Hill until his death in 1969.

Robert Carr Adams

Jerry LaGrange

Although he had a relatively short stay at Taft (11 years), Jerry LaGrange filled several important roles: Assistant to the Headmaster, Director of Admissions, Alumni Secretary, head coach of varsity football and hockey. He left in 1953 to become Headmaster of the Rye Country Day School, where he had a most successful tenure.

Bob Adams began his distinguished career at Taft immediately after graduating from Bowdoin in 1929 and devoted his life to Taft, retiring in 1970 after 41 years. He had already demonstrated his versatility at Bowdoin, where he played varsity football, ran track, and graduated Cum Laude. But like most of the schoolmasters of his generation, he was called upon to contribute his many and diverse talents to a great variety of tasks throughout his career at Taft. Except for a three year stint in the U.S. Navy in World War II, he taught History and Geography, and for many years was head coach of football and track. He succeeded Charlie Shons as Director of Athletics in 1946 and held this important job until 1963. For several years he also offered a popular course in Current Events in the Water-town Adult Education Program. In the days before computers, he was responsible for the awesome job of assembling and producing the academic schedules for students and faculty at the beginning of each school year. For many years he served as Chairman of the Middle Class Committee, and also assisted Joe Cunningham as Assistant Director of Admissions. In 1965 John Esty appointed him Dean of the Faculty, a difficult post which he filled with a fine blend of firmness and diplomacy. The first recipient (along with Toby Baker) of Taft's new sabbatical leave program, he spent his sabbatical year (1965-66) studying history at the University of North Carolina. Bob and his attractive wife Martha were a handsome and popular couple on the Taft campus, and served with grace and charm in the many different roles required of a schoolmaster and his wife in those calmer days. Named an Honorary Alumnus on Alumni Day 1970, Bob and Martha retired to the Chapel Hill they had enjoyed while on sabbatical, and where they lived until Bob's death in 1978.

Barnaby Conrad '40

Many Taft students of the 1950s thought Barney Conrad was a mythical figure. His delightful letters read in Vespers by Headmaster Cruikshank were listened to with equal measures of astonishment, disbelief and envy. After graduating from Yale in 1943, Conrad served in several U.S. consulates in Spain, where he studied bullfighting and ultimately appeared in the bull ring on the same program with Juan Belmonte, being awarded the bull's ears for his performance. His novel *Matador* (1952) grew out of this experience. After the war he served as secretary and chess companion to Sinclair Lewis, finally returning to his home port of San Francisco, where at various times he operated a restaurant, wrote twenty-six novels, founded the Santa Barbara Writers Conference, and in general lived life to the full. His son, Barnaby III '70, lives in Paris and seems to be following in his father's footsteps, having just published (in his words), "my first real book: *Absinthe, History in a Bottle*."

In the mid '40s a number of veteran faculty retired: George Wilson and Duane Robinson left in 1945, Henry Wells in 1946, and Dean McIntosh in 1947. George Wilson was head of the Math Department and had been at Taft for 33 years. Duane Robinson taught French for 17 years. After leaving Taft, he returned to his Alma Mater, Middlebury College, and is shown here in 1963 with James Armstrong '37, then President of Middlebury. A 1905 Harvard graduate, Henry Morse Wells was the well-respected head of the Modern Language Department and had been at Taft for 34 years.

Howard C. Farwell received a B.A. from Middlebury in 1913 and an M.A. from Brown in 1918. He came to Taft in 1928 after being Head of the History Department at St. Paul Academy, St. Paul, Minnesota. An excellent, but rather erratic golfer, Farwell was also a star on the faculty volley ball and bowling teams. He retired in 1954.

Memorial Service

Portrait by Deane Keller '19

On January 11, 1986, the School held a memorial service for Mr. Cruikshank. In his eulogy, Headmaster Lance Odden caught in unusually appropriate words, the character of Mr. Cruikshank and the contribution he made to Taft during his twenty-seven years.

"In these uncertain times we all need heroes and I proudly state that Paul Cruikshank was one of mine. His was a life of triumph, principle and duty never deterred by self-interest or momentary weakness.

"Images abound:

"Light burning in the headmaster's office in the early morning hours as he writes comments on every student for Miss Reilly to type or acknowledges gifts and letters from old boys by hand.

"Tea after games or church, with Edith pouring and Paul introducing people to the warmth of their home with a social grace so often absent in today's too hurried world.

"His love of words. The agony he felt each time he heard the advertisement, 'Winston tastes good like a cigarette should'...

"His love of sports, afternoon walks with Ed Douglas to watch practices and games,... forever picking up papers, gesturing with his hands as he talked.

"The fear and trembling his surprise visits to corridors struck in the hearts of students and faculty alike. Could we ever meet his standards?

"The clarity of his vespers. The importance of the hymn, 'Now the day is over'...

"Not only did he lead us back from debt and the Depression, but he also took us through two wars, established a new order of academic excellence in the 1950's, built count-less facilities, an extraordinary faculty — many of whom went on to lead their own schools — and perhaps most important of all, he reinforced Taft's belief in student responsibility and initiative as he introduced elected monitors, the work program, the honor system, our word as our bond, living principled lives.

"Sometimes he irritated us because he was so concerned about the little details of life: dress, appearance, manners, neatness, punctuality. He did so because he believed we were better than we thought we were ourselves. He did so because he believed that if you took care of the annoying, petty details of life, if you demonstrated self-discipline and a concern for others, then the big decisions and challenges would take care of themselves. You would follow the right course.

"Paul Cruikshank believed the disciplined person was the one prepared to serve his family, society, and to make the world a better place. No one could have been a finer example. He never asked of us what he had not already done himself. Paul Cruikshank made us grow. He challenged each of us to be a better person. To count."

JOHN C. ESTY, JR.
HEADMASTER 1963—1972

John Esty — Taft's Third Headmaster

On February 11, 1963, the Board of Trustees announced that John Cushing Esty, Jr., would succeed Paul Cruikshank as Taft's third Headmaster. At the time, Mr. Esty was Associate Dean and Instructor in Mathematics at Amherst College. Brought up in Chappaqua, New York, he graduated from Deerfield Academy and went on to Amherst, graduating Magna Cum Laude in 1950. He received a master's degree from Yale in 1951 and also did graduate work at the University of California at Berkeley. From 1951 to 1953 he served in the U.S. Air Force as a First Lieutenant, returning to Amherst after his military service. At Amherst he was at various times Assistant Director of Admissions and, as Associate Dean since 1957, had been in charge of the Freshman Program, in this capacity obtaining an excellent insight into the secondary school field. He was married to Katharine Cole, daughter of the president of Amherst, and the couple had three boys at the time they came to Watertown.

From the beginning, John Esty made it clear that he was "180 degrees different from Paul Cruikshank," and before he began to establish his own program, one of the first things he did upon arriving at Taft was to try to get to know his faculty. Nearly each faculty member received a formal summons to come to the Headmaster's office for a "get-acquainted" talk. Although the hour was scheduled in a formal manner, the actual talk was very informal (Mr. Esty perched on the side of his desk) — in a way in which faculty appearances seldom had been in the same office a year earlier.

In a similar move on the student level, Mr. Esty arranged to be in his office — with the door open — every afternoon from 5:00 to 6:00, available to any student who wished to come in "to talk."

The Editor's Personal Recollections

A personal recollection may be illuminating. When Mr. Esty's appointment was announced, I was the Director of Public Relations —responsible for all news releases and school publications. As such, I wrote to Mr. Esty at Amherst, asking for biographical information and photographs to help prepare an appropriate news release. In my letter, I mentioned something about "you can see the problems a Public Relations officer faces." John Esty's response was typical of his forthright approach: "You speak of problems; I see only solutions."

He *was* different from Mr. Cruikshank, and one of the earliest departures from routine was the change in the format of Vespers. Under Mr. Cruikshank, Vespers was a formal, dignified service. Held in the beautiful Bingham Auditorium, Vespers started promptly each evening except Saturday at 6:00 p.m. "Promptly" meant when the six o'clock bell finished ringing — at

which time the auditorium doors were closed by the School monitors — often in the face of late-comers, rushing down the corridor. (They had to find their way to the balcony, where their names were duly noted, and they were given "Late to Vespers" demerits.)

The Monitors then proceeded in stately fashion down the aisles, sitting at the end of alternate rows, where they took attendance. The stage was set with two chairs and a podium. As one faced the stage, the chair on the left was occupied by the speaker of the evening — usually the Headmaster. On the right — the so-called "Amen Corner" — sat a senior master, whose task it was to announce the hymn and start the Lord's Prayer at the close of the service.

After the monitors had settled in their seats, the speaker arose, walked to the podium, and delivered his remarks. Usually lasting 10 or 15 minutes (anything much longer could be described as bravery above and beyond the call of duty), the talk was serious, although not necessarily religious, in tone. At the end of the talk, the speaker returned to his chair; the faculty member in the Amen Corner then rose and announced the number of the evening hymn. He then sat down again. As the organist neared the end of the hymn's prelude, the master rose again, as did the audience. At the conclusion of the singing — often faint-hearted at best — the master commenced intoning the Lord's Prayer. This was no easy feat. The Seniors in the front row delighted in trying to throw him off stride — especially a new master in his first turns in the Amen Corner. In the first place, they riveted their eyes on

Katharine Esty is introduced to the Alumni on Alumni Day 1963.

"Walking It Off": J.V. cross country runner David Hudson '65 is assisted by varsity runner Andy Larkin '64 as he "walks off" after a race.

him in an unnerving, unsettling stare. They never commenced with "Our Father..." at once, but let the poor suffering fellow on the platform fumble with these opening phrases which must be among the most-often recited in the language. (Several masters have been known to bring to the platform a typewritten version of the Lord's Prayer, so that they would be saved from an absolutely complete black-out.) Having finally completed his task, the master must remember to leave the hymnal in the chair, then walk down from the platform, up the aisle, and out of the Auditorium, followed seriatim, by the boys (Seniors first), who politely waited for faculty wives and guests to come out of the last rows of seats.

All of this by way of preamble.

On the afternoon in question, I chanced to meet Mr. Esty in the hall. He asked me if I were going to Vespers that evening.

"Yes, I usually do, why?"

"You may see something really different tonight."

"What?"

"Wait and see," he said with a mischievous grin. "But be there."

The first thing one noticed that evening was that the stage was bare. Gone were the two lovely corner chairs and the elaborate podium. The platform was absolutely barren. All of the usual routine was followed: the Monitors came down the aisles and settled in their seats. An expectant hush fell over the curious boys — always quick to notice deviations from routine.

The curtain parted in the middle, and the Headmaster emerged, carrying a straight-back chair and — a GUITAR.

Deftly he placed the chair in the center of the stage, sat down with guitar at ready, and announced:

"Gentlemen, tonight I am going to sing for you; and then I want you to sing for me."

With that, he began to sing one of the most popular protest songs of the year: "Blowin' in the Wind." The silence at the end was excruciating. No one knew whether or not to applaud. (The student tradition had been that no speech by an in-house master was ever applauded — presumably on the grounds that it might be embarrassing to applaud greatly some particularly good talk and much less vigorously for a long and boring talk.) In any event, nothing happened. Then the Headmaster asked the congregation to join him in the chorus. He started again — and again it was ominously quiet. I must confess my own recollections are somewhat blurred at this point because of my own intense embarrassment and confusion. As I recall it, a few brave souls managed to emit some quavering notes, and gradually a fairly respectable response came from the crowd — although it never approached a whole-hearted chorus.

Mr. Esty's gesture was worthy of Cyrano de Bergerac. Taft singing *had* been poor — listless and apathetic. And Mr. Esty had two things in his background that made him more than usually sensitive to the value of vigorous male singing: Deerfield (his own preparatory school) had a strong tradition of student singing, and secondly, he himself possessed a fine baritone voice. I would guess also that his attempt was prompted by the belief that group singing was a marvelous way to unite a school and to start communication. A courageous and sincere attempt had been made to vitalize a worthy but tired tradition. The attempt was only partially successful, but it laid the ground for future, no less startling breaks with the past.

Photo by Marvin Koner, courtesy of Fortune magazine.

TAFT ALUMNI CITATION OF MERIT

ROBERT ALPHONSO TAFT '06

Scholar, member of the Bar, leader of men, outstanding member of a family renowned throughout the nation in all generations for its public service, state representative, Speaker of the House of Representatives of Ohio, United States Senator from Ohio from 1939 until his death, creator of responsible, constructive political leadership, whose memorials are not only of stone and sounding bells but in a standard of public conduct and integrity unmatched in our nation's history coupled with a practical knowledge which has made real his vision. He was the rare statesman who could command by sheer respect rather than retribution and who possessed not only the judgment but the courage to confess error and doubt. His personality and the compelling force of his concepts are some of the landmarks of our free society now and for all time.

John Esty Presents His Case

John Esty is an amazingly articulate man. Both on paper and at the podium, he expresses himself with clarity and force. It is impossible in the brief space available to do justice to his numerous speeches and essays, but the excerpts that follow will give a rough idea of some of the topics that interested him over the years of his headmastership.

In his first speech to the Taft alumni on Alumni Day 1963, he touched briefly on an aspect of adolescent behaviour that would be a recurring concern: The "Identity Crisis" of a youngster trying to "find himself." Starting with a reference to Stephen Dedalus in *Portrait of the Artist as a Young Man,* Mr. Esty showed how painful it is to confront the "bewildering adult world." "Understanding and aiding the process of self-identity is the major problem of schools and colleges in the mid-20th century. The best answer, or at least the first clue, lies in what the Taft School has always done instinctively — that is, to provide a firm intellectual and social structure as a base of security for an increasing number of forays into new knowledge and new awareness of self. (The Taft program) implies both conservation of traditional values and liberation of individual growth impulses.... We must seek new insights, admit new knowledge, experiment with new methods, and be willing to accept new forms of old truths."

Mr. Esty's opening remarks to the Taft faculty in September 1963 expanded on these ideas. Acknowledging his debt to John Gardner,* the Headmaster elaborated on the concept of an "ever-renewing society." He

A typically informal John Esty mode of transportation.

started by suggesting the factors that inhibit renewal:
1) fear of new ideas
2) academic conservatism
3) vested interests
4) over-organization

He then enumerated and enlarged on the qualities of the "self-renewing man:"
1) maturity
2) tolerance
3) individuality
4) versatility
5) energy and enthusiasm
6) the discovery of self
7) a free society

The Saturday Review, 5 January 1963

Taft would get an A on some aspects of the ever-renewing society (summer study plan) and flunk others (rules and regulations). What changes will the Headmaster make? None. The changes "will be generated from within the society, mostly by the faculty. . . . If we can discover our own individual potentialities for growth and renewal, then our direction and destiny will establish itself. . . The Headmaster's role will be simple. Alexander the Great once called on the great teacher, Diogenes, and asked what he could do for him. Diogenes replied: "Only stand out of my light."

A year later the Headmaster's opening remarks to the faculty began with a typical Esty gambit: start with an eye-opener. In this case it was to challenge some of the most revered tenets of private school education: the traditional goals of "building character," developing good study habits, espousing the virtues of hard work.

He then went on to say that he was challenging such ideas but not rejecting them. For example, hard work is a virtue only when it leads to some achievement.

To what end *should* the faculty bend its efforts?

1) The clarification of experience. The art of the teacher is "to alternate vivid experience with reflective clarification, to present students with a series of events which are made understandable and relevant to their lives."

2) The establishment of self-esteem. "The strength to be an individual and the search for one's identity depend above all on the development of self-esteem. . . . The teacher must always be ready to

In 1967 Dick Geldard '53 produced *A Thousand Clowns,* with Bob Sweet '68 in the lead, and Andy Jamieson '67 as Murray Burns' long-suffering conventional brother.

praise and reinforce the slightest impulse toward growth."

Undoubtedly the most controversial essay Mr. Esty produced was the one in which he established a Long Range Planning Committee to study Taft's future. It was in this proposal that he stated: "The fundamental reason for the work of this Committee is my belief that *during the next 25 years all but a few leading private secondary schools will vanish.* (his italics) Only those which are already strong and which plan now for their future shape and financial strength will have a chance for survival."

During his four years at Taft Steve Sherer '57 created many fine cartoons and caricatures for school publications. Perhaps most memorable is his "Faculty Crossing the Delaware".

Faculty in the '60s and '70s

It soon became apparent that the faculty would not escape the turmoil of the 1960s. The restlessness (nay, rebelliousness) of the students was obviously a strain on the common bond between teacher and pupil — that is, the striving together toward a mutually-desirable goal — the education of the student. It seemed that the partners in the enterprise no longer shared common concerns in pursuit of this goal. The first skirmish arose over the question of "relevance." While subjects such as Latin and Greek had long been under attack on this basis, the debate now engaged subjects such as English and History. It seemed that anything written before 1960 was totally "irrelevant." Novels such as *The Mayor of Casterbridge* were displaced by *One Flew Over*

the Cuckoo's Nest. The entire curriculum was under scrutiny, but at the moment, we will examine its impact on the faculty.

The senior masters bore the brunt of the upheaval. Reared in traditions of self-discipline, respect for authority, and the virtues of hard work, these men were suddenly told that such values meant little to the new breed of students. The ugly battle cry, "Don't trust anyone over thirty!" badly wounded many of these men who had heretofore treasured a close association with their young charges. Of course all of them had cheerfully accepted the fact that to the fifteen-year old anyone in his late twenties or early thirties was "ancient." But there had been a friendliness, a mutual respect, an aura of give and take that enabled the two — master and student — to work together and to form bonds that varied widely with the different individuals but which nonetheless were widespread in the best schools of the forties and fifties.

Aside from the personal level, there was the matter of professional judgment — of hard-won experience that was early called into question in these unhappy days. Men who had spent years acquiring a considerable body of knowledge — both in formal study at graduate school and in their own classrooms — now found that there seemed to be little market for such knowledge.

It should be remembered that these senior faculty members were not all men who lived entirely by the book or were hide-bound old fogies. They themselves were independent souls — men who had, perhaps, chosen the teaching profession because of the freedom or latitude they thought it would provide. True, they had to work within a certain framework — the department syllabus or the over-all philosophy of the school. But once inside his own classroom a teacher had a degree of personal freedom that not many men in the business world found until they reached top management levels. Despite the fact that many were registered Republicans, many of them were liberal in their thinking. (My own conservative brothers-in-law used to call me "that pinko school teacher" when we got together at family reunions.)

It is not surprising, then, that the school lost several fine senior masters during this era. This is not to attribute such losses entirely to the turmoil of the times, but it does seem likely that battle fatigue (or to use a later, more fashion-able phrase, "teacher burn-out") was a contributing factor in many cases.

Schools are, by their very nature, an ever-renewing social order. In the ordinary course the student body rotates every four years. And faculty come and go for a variety of reasons. But during the nine years of John Esty's headmastership, there were some peculiarly significant departures, in both faculty and staff.

- George Morgan retired in June 1963 after forty years.
- Robert Woolsey resigned that same year to become Headmaster of the Casady School in Oklahoma City.
- Fred Clark resigned in 1964 to become Headmaster of the Cate School, Carpinteria, California.
- Catherine Grant, the school nurse for 30 years, retired in the fall of 1964.
- P.T. Young, Chairman of the Music Department, resigned in 1965.
- Dr. Edwin Reade, long-time school doctor, retired in 1967.
- Harry Stearns retired in 1967 after 38 years.

1969 was a particularly difficult year.
- James P. Logan died in February 1969.
- Paul Lovett-Janison retired in June 1969.
- Leonard Sargent resigned at the same time.
- William Sullivan died in November 1969.
- Superintendent of Buildings James Hanning retired in 1970.
- George Gould died in 1970.

All of these twelve men and the one woman had contributed greatly to the Taft School, and all left their mark.

George and Nora Morgan

In his eleven years at Taft, Bob Woolsey provided an "intellectual spark" for the faculty and students. The fact that he had a Ph.D. from Yale (rather rare in secondary schools in those days) and that his subject field was Greek and Latin undoubtedly lent a certain cachet to his role in the school. But there was nothing phony about his credentials — or about the man himself. He had a genuine interest in intellectual matters and worked effectively to encourage similar interest at the school. His founding of the Faculty Lecture Series prodded many on the faculty to produce "learned" papers that otherwise would never have been written. In addition to his duties at Taft, Mr. Woolsey was also an active member of Christ Episcopal Church in Watertown and an effective layman in the Episcopal Diocese of Connecticut. His impact on the school may perhaps be best exemplified by the fact that the 1964 *Annual* (a year *after* his departure) devoted a full page to him "In Remembrance."

George Morgan had been at Taft for 40 years, most of the time as Head of the Music Department. In addition to his "in-house" duties as Director of the Glee Club and (until 1949) the Concert Band, he also organized several outside musical activities, most prominently, the Spring Choral Festivals and the Five School Concerts. In the Watertown area, he founded the Choristers and was active with the Waterbury Symphony Orchestra. His wife Nora, a talented singer and teacher, annually helped produce the fine Christmas Choir programs. Affectionately known to many of the earlier classes as "Red," Mr. Morgan was a skilled concert pianist, and each year his several piano recitals in Vespers gave the boys an opportunity to hear many classical and modern compositions. He and Mrs. Morgan always welcomed boys into their home and, as the *Papyrus* said in its comment on their retirement: "The Morgans will always be remembered for their great personal warmth and genuine enthusiasm."

Robert Woolsey

P.T. Young

Phillip Taylor Young (always known to one and all as "P.T.") came to Taft in 1949 straight out of Bowdoin College. In his sixteen years at Taft he did a great deal to develop the instrumental side of music at the school. With boundless energy — "zest" is really the word to describe his manner — he put together a variety of musical organizations from the concert band to a very proficient jazz band, in the process overcoming obstacles that would have daunted a less energetic and vigorous man. The 1965 *Annual* described him in several apt phrases: "...he enlivened music at Taft with his voluminous wit and forceful manner... a perennial favorite with the mothers (as conductor of the Concert Band)...his teaching has a forceful vigor and depth that make his classes always rewarding and often very humorous." An early exponent of the "do-it-yourself" philosophy, P.T. built a harpsichord for the school and a cabin for his family on an island in Lake Winnepe-

saukee, N.H. He left to become Assistant Head of the Yale School of Music.

Catherine Grant's retirement in October 1964 marked not only the end of her own 30 years of service, but in many ways (trite as it may sound) the end of an era. She had served under all three of Taft's Headmasters: Mr. Taft, Mr. Cruikshank, and Mr. Esty, and was as close to being "an institution" within the larger "institution" as is possible. In her domain, known with the unerring instinct of youth as "Grant's Tomb", she was "one of the few remaining absolute monarchs" as Dr. Richard Stock '41 observed in his remarks upon the occasion of her retirement. In the all-male world of her day, she provided (along with a few faculty wives) a feminine presence and warmth much appreciated — if unspoken — by countless ill and homesick boys. The warmth was concealed by her "no nonsense" exterior (the *Papyrus* noted the "iron hand" with which she ruled the Infirmary), but as the *Pap* continued, "Although her tyranny is legend,...her 'bark is worse than her bite'." Her own inimitable trademark was her practice of baking double layer chocolate cakes for birthdays of faculty children and boys who spent their birthday in the infirmary. Faculty wives made a thoughtful gift to Catherine upon her departure by presenting her with a photograph album containing the pictures of faculty children who had been happy recipients of her cakes over the years. The Taft Alumni Association also rendered her the signal honor of electing her an "honorary alumna" of the school.

Dr. Edwin G. Reade, the school doctor for 22 years, retired in the fall of 1967. He had succeeded Dr. James Martin, Taft's first physician, and was in turn succeeded by Dr. William Bassford, thus giving the school a parallel distinction to its having had only three head-

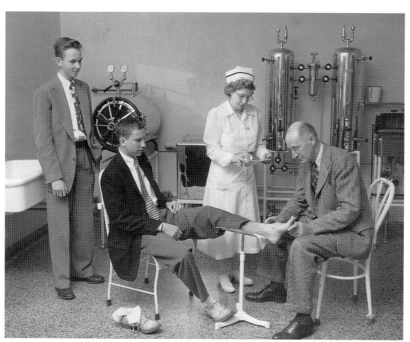

Dr. Reade and Catherine Grant

masters at the time. Ed Douglas recorded Dr. Reade's contributions to Taft in the Alumni Bulletin. "Broken bones, cuts, concussions, contusions, colds, measles, mumps, chicken pox, and the problem of those who simply wanted to get 'off ex' were all a part of his day. . . . He recognized the 'faker' quickly but sensed the seriousness of what on the surface appeared to be only a minor problem. . . . His very calmness and patience brought reassurance to many a bedside in the Martin Infirmary." Always known as "Brownie", Dr. Reade delivered virtually all of the Taft faculty children during his years in the community. He and his wife Trudi had two sons, both Taft alumni: Edwin G. (Jr.) '39, and Robert '43.

James P. Logan died in February 1969 in Pompano Beach, Florida. Ill for some time, Jim had been granted a leave of absence for the academic year and had been living in Florida not far from Albert Fusonie, former Taft master and long-time friend. Hired by Mr. Taft in

1933, Jim was in many ways the epitome of the legendary "schoolmaster." A bachelor, Jim saw his role at Taft going far beyond being simply a teacher of Physics and a basketball coach — although he was good at both. Today's catch phrase — "a role model" — best describes Jim's way of life. He set high standards — on the playing field, at the dining table, in the classroom. Always immaculately dressed, he hated sloppiness in any form — dress, thinking, speech. In his wryly humorous way he delighted in impressing one with the importance of precision in speech. To the question: "Do you have a cigarette?", he would slowly and deliberately extract his pack from his breast pocket, peer inside, and then replace it, saying calmly: "Yes." The rather non-plussed would-be-borrower soon learned to ask Jim, *"May* I have a cigarette, please." But he was not stuffy. Even the above incident was always accompanied by a warm smile, and his reputation for being an inveterate punster was widespread. Faculty members knew him as a genial host and a marvelous addition to a dinner party. He loved to play games and was a past master at Charades. Jim's longtime friend and former Taft master, Gerald LaGrange, headmaster of the Rye Country Day School, made perceptive comments on Jim at the occasion of the dedication of the Logan Field House, Alumni Day 1972. "Jim counted himself fortunate to be a part of the Taft School, and he was immensely proud of the fact that he was associated with this institution. . . . He felt privileged to have the opportunity to render service to this school and its students, and considered his work at Taft most rewarding in itself. . . . He did not find the regulated routine and cloistered environment irksome or restrictive. Rather, as a

James Logan

ness was a noteworthy trait —one that served him well in the classroom. To quote the 1965 *Annual:* "His classes are often grueling ordeals because when Mr. L-J gets in front of the blackboard nothing interrupts his concentration. This trait, combined with an almost overwhelming knowledge of the sciences, make the forty-five minute sessions far from boring note-taking, but rather an insight into the intricate and yet highly-ordered world of the natural sciences." And the 1969 Annual Dedication called him "a source of academic excellence and inspiration...A proud figure in his white lab smock, L-J continues to meet the highest standards in chemistry and physics. Our thanks for twenty-seven years of timeless dignity." Paul never lost his sharp English accent, and he and his wife Elaine were a most gregarious couple, hosting some memorable faculty dinner parties.

highly organized person, he relished living on an ordered schedule..." A natural athlete, Jim was a superior coach of a variety of sports and produced many championship teams — particularly in basketball. Naming the new field house in his honor appropriately preserves his contribution to the school.

Paul Lovett-Janison retired in 1969 after twenty-seven years at Taft. Born in England, he graduated from Sheffield University and earned a Ph.D. in Chemistry at Columbia in 1940. A stickler for good manners at the dining room table, he had been known to use his knife to whack the hand of any student who reached for the bread tray without first offering it to "the head of the table." Legend has it that he broke many a glass while setting his high standards for good manners at the table. His single-minded-

Paul Lovett-Janison

The death of Bill Sullivan in November 1969 shocked the Taft community. In Groton, Massachusetts, to watch his son Jay, Captain of the Groton football team, play against Milton Academy, Mr. Sullivan suffered a massive cerebral hemorrhage and died in the Groton Community Hospital. Although he spent most of his last years as an administrator, his greatest talent and his first love was teaching. The 1965 Annual carried this appraisal: "As a teacher, Mr. Sullivan possesses rare gifts. His own intense love for his subject provides an atmosphere which makes one of his classes an inspiring experience. His sharp wit and sensitive approach to whatever he teaches set him apart as a truly great schoolmaster." Significantly, he was the first recipient of the School's Mailliard Award for Excellence in Teaching in 1959 and again received the award in 1964. Although he was by no means a great athlete, Bill was always proud of his coaching of the "Little Giants", the Lower Mid and Mid football team of the forties and fifties. Very active in the various professional aspects of his career, he was for many years an English Reader of the College Entrance Examination Board and a member of the School and College Conference in English. In his Memorial remarks, John Esty summed up Bill's essential characteristics: "Bill Sullivan's vision of greatness for Taft derived from his own great energy, talents, drive, integrity, and spirit. His restless personal vitality was immense. ... The bursting bigness of his life is the measure of the huge emptiness of the space left behind. His wit, his puckish view of things, the richness of his language always seemed uniquely Celtic to me." Bill's widow, Marietta, continued the Sullivan tradition at Taft as teacher of Remedial English until her own death in 1982.

William E. Sullivan

February 1968: Lt. Joe Knowlton '64, recipient of the Bronze Star, in Vietnam.

Leonard Sargent

The student protests of the '60s and '70s were gathering steam. Rick DeVillafranca '68 caught some of the spirit of the times in this Papyrus cartoon.

Leonard R. Sargent

After 32 years at Taft, Leonard Sargent surprised the school community by his premature retirement in 1969. A mathematics instructor whose prime interest was hockey, Sargent was known as the "Winter God," and was responsible for Taft's building the Mays Rink. Year after year he led successful Taft hockey teams to victories in the Housatonic Valley League as well as post-season tournaments such as the Lawrenceville Invitational Tournament. He came to Taft in 1937, immediately after graduation from Princeton and served in the U.S. Navy as a Lt. Commander from 1942-46. After he left Taft, Sargent married and retired to his Montana ranch. His carefully reasoned, thoughtfully expressed letter of resignation captures some of the "down side" of the turmoil being experienced by the school during those disturbing times and is worth extensive quotation:

"Why, after all these most enjoyable and rewarding years at Taft, has the profession lost its charms? The cause is definitely not Taft in particular, as I feel we here are meeting the challenge of the times as well as and better than most schools. . . The change has been in the boys — or more specifically, the mores of the times as reflected in the boys — not in all of them , of course, or even in the majority, but in too many cases. . . It would seem that suddenly traditions are dead (or very sick) — patriotism, honor, manners, good taste, even cleanliness. If an ideal were ever revered, it is now reviled . . . I am confident that the present attitude of youth is a temporary phase. Even now, I do not think it represents more than a small but noisy segment of the age. It may, however, take some time for the pendulum to swing, and after 32 years of great pleasure and satisfaction in teaching and coaching, I do not want to take the chance of souring while waiting for this change. . . I hope my resignation will have at least one constructive effect: youth might benefit from the realization that they are not the only ones who think they feel strongly. Some of us oldsters have ideals, too — and are so dedicated that they are willing to give up their way of life and profession rather than watch the degradation of these values, traditions, and ideals."

John Esty and Seniors
exchanging views — 1970.

Independent Studies

The Independent Studies Program was John Esty's earliest and most innovative contribution to the academic side of school life. First outlined in the spring of 1964, it was set in place that fall, with Lance Odden as Director.*

The original proposal made to Upper Middlers and Middlers in the spring of 1964 outlined the following objects of the program:

    1) To encourage boys with talent and/or interest to undertake projects that will challenge and stimulate them.

    2) To allow these boys the opportunity to do genuinely "independent" work under the general guidance of a faculty tutor.

    3) To free "mature" boys from some of the usual requirements of school life.

The last point had perhaps the most dramatic impact on the students. In essence, it meant that they did not have to attend classes; were excused from the job program and athletics; and did not have to complete course work in the field in which their independent project was concerned. Another attractive feature was provided by accommodating all of the ISP students in the former Cruikshank residence with few corridor restrictions — such as "lights." In return for these privileges, the students were expected to complete all regular course work, take some form of regular exercise, and "behave like mature individuals."

The response of the students was immediate and positive. Nearly one quarter of the Upper Middle Class made tentative applications for the fall term.

*History teacher Fred Clark — one of the founding fathers of the Independent Studies Program — was originally named first Director of the Program. But Mr. Clark left Taft in the summer of 1964 to become Headmaster of the Cate School in Carpinteria, California. Mr. Odden was named to succeed him.

Alumni Day 1969: Mrs. Hulbert Taft, Jr., assists in the cornerstone ceremony for the new library named in memory of her late husband, a member of the class of 1926. Left, her son Dudley Taft '58; center, Headmaster Esty.

Among the first ten ISP participants were the following: a student exploring the writings of Martin Buber; a musician giving a recital on the French horn; a student teacher in Spanish; a budding playwright; and two students investigating — respectively — the writings of C.S. Lewis and Gerard Manley Hopkins. At the conclusion of this first term's program one of the participants declared in the *Papyrus* that the program was a "resounding success." The participants gained "a deep sense of personal satisfaction and demonstrated that conscientious students are able to live up to the responsibilities as well as the freedoms of individual study."

Another feature of the Independent Studies Program that proved most stimulating to the entire school was the presence on campus of a number of distinguished "outsiders" who visited the school to serve as an inspiration or spark to the participants in the program. Over the years the school was fortunate to have speakers such as Robert Penn Warren, Archibald MacLeish, Mildred

Dunnock, and a host of distinguished professors from a variety of universities.

The variety of projects undertaken in the Independent Studies Program has been far beyond the imagination of the originators of the program in its formative stage. At the risk of presenting just a dull list of projects, it may still be worthwhile and instructive to note some of the areas that students elected to pursue at various times:

In the *literary* field, for example, students made some sort of attempt to grapple with: D.H. Lawrence, Gerard Manley Hopkins, Franz Kafka, Dylan Thomas, Edward Albee, Garcia Lorca, e.e. cummings, Thomas Hardy. On the "creative" side, students wrote plays, poetry, and novelettes.

In the *sciences,* students explored such diverse areas as physical meteorology, grinding a 16″ telescope mirror, investigating pollution in the Taft pond, laser optics, and the effect of drugs on the nervous system of sea horses.

In the *social sciences:* an analysis of Chinese Communist foreign policy, a study of migrating workers, the crash of 1929, American foreign policy in Latin America, Fidel Castro's rise to power, and Soviet foreign policy in the 1920s.

Miscellaneous: constructing a harpsichord, building a model of a girls' school on the Taft campus, writing a series of computer programs for non-mathematical applications, translating Aesop's fables from the Greek, translating Medieval Latin manuscripts, a study of American blues music. In addition, there were numerous student teaching interns: seniors who taught Lower Mid (and Mid) classes in virtually every school discipline.

It was not long before the concept of the Independent Study Program began to spread beyond the original area. In 1967, the English Department took the lead in extending the spirit of the ISP program into other areas of the curriculum by announcing an experimental two-week project for all Upper Mids at the end of the Winter Term. Well in advance, each instructor announced a particular aspect of literature upon which he intended to concentrate.

The options offered were the works of Hardy and Conrad, the theme of isolation in European literature, the theme of isolation in American literature, and a study of satire. Students elected one of the areas and met with the individual instructor singly or in small groups during the two-week period. At the end of the time, each student submitted a written research paper or participated in a panel discussion of the works he had examined.

During this time the regularly-scheduled Upper Middle English classes did not meet. The experimental nature of the project carried over into the grading, for the projects were graded in a more "general" manner than usual, receiving one of three grades: honors, pass, or unsatisfactory. Both faculty and students thought the experiment generally successful and worthwhile.

An appealing minor aspect of the ISP program was the attempt to give more scholarly prestige to the projects by binding each final paper in hard cover and placing it in the archives of the school library. Although this practice continued for a number of years, it was gradually abandoned because of the immense diversity of projects that did not lend themselves readily to such a practice — building a harpsichord, for example.

The program as a whole attracted considerable attention in the academic community at large, and Taft received numerous inquiries from other schools who wished to start similar programs. Without doubt, Mr. Esty's pioneering program was one of those concepts that came off at just the right time — hitting

Alumni Day 1969: "Spank" Sheldon '39 arrives in his 1911 fire truck, which he shows off here to classmates Bill Moore, Len Myers, Charles Hungerford, and their wives.

a responsive note with students, faculty, parents, and trustees. It was indeed "a resounding success."

The Independent Studies Program has proved to be a hardy plant. Twenty-three years later it was still alive and thriving. Barclay Johnson '53, English Instructor and for many years Director of the ISP, reported in June 1987 that the past year had been an "outstanding year with more completed projects of a higher quality than we've had in the last twenty years." Projects ranged from an "Insider's Guide to Taft," which will help new students adjust to Taft more quickly by describing daily life at the school, to a study of the history of rocketry and a study of investments listed on the New York Stock Exchange. Many projects were arts-related, such as an historical study of Goya's art, advanced work in batik, and original plays. At graduation two Goldberg awards are presented for distinguished projects; in short, this program that was so innovative in 1964 has become an established part of the education at Taft.

During the sixties, changes in the pattern of religious observances were among the first significant breaks with the past. Although Taft had never been a church-related school, a serious respect for religion had always been an important part of school life. A School Chaplain had been a member of the faculty virtually since the beginning of the school.

In the 1950s, an evening Vespers service was held six nights a week (not Saturday). Attendance at Sunday church was compulsory. All students except Catholics and Jews, who attended services at their own places of worship, were expected to attend the 9:00 a.m. service at Christ Church (Episcopal) on the Green. Although attendance was compulsory, and therefore immediately suspect in the eyes of the boys, the services were, in fact, not always dull and boring. A different clergyman spoke each week, and the sermons were different from the usual Sunday morning 11:00 o'clock variety offered by the average small-town pastor. The boys never knew how lucky they were. (Masters, too, were expected to attend at least one service a month.) But the old adage "You can lead a horse to water..." never had more truth. Various attempts were made by the boys to enliven the proceedings, the most memorable being the weekly race to see which acolyte could extinguish his candles first. Taking place at the very end of the service, this contest drew all eyes, despite the fact that the kneeling congregation was supposedly engrossed in prayer, eyes closed in religious contemplation. In fact, the tension was audible as the acolytes, candle-snuffers in hand, moved to the altar, and then parted company — one to one side, the other to the other side. The race was not always to the swift; occasionally one might be one candle ahead of his com-

The Sunday Schedule and Vespers

Wednesday, December 3, 1969, was library moving day. The entire student body, faculty, and faculty wives were involved in the move, which in four hours shifted nearly 25,000 books from the Woolworth Library in Charles Phelps Taft Hall to the new Hulbert Taft, Jr. Library.

patriot, when one of the candles he thought he had successfully extinguished re-ignited itself, and he had to backtrack to complete the job. The reason for the haste was that the extinguishing of the final candle signified the end of the service, and the congregation was released from bondage. Were bets ever placed on the outcome of this little contest? Heaven forbid!

In the first month of his administration, September 1963, Mr. Esty began to restructure the Sunday schedule. Prior to 1963, the Sunday program was — like the rest of the school routine — fixed in a series of prescribed events. In a slight concession to the rigorous weekday schedule, Sunday breakfast was delayed from 7:00 a.m. to 8:00 a.m. (The unlucky waiters at Sunday breakfast still had to eat *their* breakfast before serving the rest of the school.)

Theoretically, a bit of free time ensued after the 9:00 a.m. church service, but in fact this period was frequently used for Corridor Committee meetings and other necessary administrative obligations. The main meal of the day was at 1:00 p.m. with white table cloths on the dining room tables and a more elaborate menu. Afterwards, coffee was served for the faculty in the Cruikshank apartment. Again, some free time was technically available after lunch, although Lower Mids and Mids had required exercise, and Lower Mids were expected to write a weekly letter home during this time. Vespers was at 6:00 p.m., followed by another sit-down dinner. For all of these occurrences, boys were expected to be dressed appropriately — in practice, a gray-flannel or dark blue suit.

To Mr. Esty, this program seemed unnecessarily restricted and fragmented.

Dr. Henry Sage Fenimore Cooper '13 and Mrs. Cooper shortly after he received the Alumni Citation of Merit, May 1969.

Joe Cunningham, in his role as Director of Admissions, annually enlivened first faculty meetings with wry assessments of the admissions scene. His superb timing, his mumbled recital of percentages, say, from private schools versus public schools, his obvious sincerity hidden behind a veil of humor, and his unshakable belief that the Taft faculty could, if they would, bring out the best in each of his human offerings, made his annual appearance a not-to-be-missed event for his colleagues on the faculty.

Valedictorian of his class at Mercersburg Academy, Joe graduated with High Honors from Princeton in 1933, and received his M.A. from Harvard a year later. Teaching first at the Northwood School, Lake Placid, he spent several summers studying in France and came to Taft in 1937. With the exception of WW II service as a sergeant in the Signal Corps, he spent the rest of his career at Taft, serving in a variety of roles: Dean, Director of Admissions, Assistant Headmaster, and of course teacher of French, retiring in 1976. Joe's wife Betty carried on the spirit of Edith Cruikshank, keeping the halls filled with flowers and serving as gracious hostess at innumerable teas. Their retirement home on Guernseytown Road overlooks the campus and keeps them in close harmony with the school to which Joe devoted his life for so many years.

He felt that both students and faculty needed a longer stretch of time that was "unstructured" — free from required attendance — time that they could use in any way they saw fit.

His first step was to eliminate Sunday Vespers. Although a seemingly small move, its effect was to let Sunday permissions run until 7:30 p.m. — a change that provided an extra hour and a half of free time.

A year later, in the fall term of 1964, further adjustments were made to the Sunday schedule. The principal change was to move required church service from 9:00 a.m. to 5:00 p.m. The service was also moved from Christ Church to the Congregational Church and greater latitude was given in the selection of a church to attend. Attendance at a church service was required, but a student could attend any church of his choice: Methodist, Lutheran, Episcopalian, Catholic, etc.

Perhaps of even greater significance to the boys, breakfast and lunch were no longer required meals. What all of these changes meant was simply that a greater portion of Sunday and Saturday was "free" — free from required attendance at various set times and free from traditional dress requirements. If a student was not involved in a major athletic commitment, he was relatively free from after Saturday lunch until 5:00 p.m. Sunday. Needless to say, all of these changes were extremely popular.

Ed Douglas served Taft for 42 years as math teacher, Track coach, Dean, and Assistant Headmaster. His quickness on the athletic field was echoed in his quickness of speech and in his no-nonsense approach to the daily, mostly small-scale, problems of boarding school life.

Always proud of his Brooklyn heritage, Ed did his undergraduate work at Hamilton College, where he won five varsity letters in track and cross-country and graduated Phi Beta Kappa. Immediately after obtaining his M.A. from Harvard in 1931, he came to Taft to begin his long career, interrupted only by a three-year WW II stint in the Army, emerging as master sergeant. In addition to his numerous duties at Taft, Ed served in a variety of roles outside the school, principally as a member of the CEEB Commission of Mathematics and as President of the Connecticut Association of Independent Schools. A tour of India as a Math consultant rounded out Ed's 25 years as Chairman of the Math Department, and he ended his career as holder of the Independence Foundation Chair. Retiring in 1974, Ed and wife Jean moved to a small house in Watertown, where Ed pursued his hobby of gardening. He died there in May 1976.

Changes in the Vespers Format

During this time, the format of the daily Vespers service also underwent considerable change. Under Mr. Cruikshank, the Headmaster was basically responsible for the evening service, with a senior master assigned to the Amen Corner. Ordinarily, one did not become a member of this elite group until one received "tenure" — usually after five years — although some exceptional beings were given the opportunity of serving after three years. The nights of the week had a pattern: Monday, Tuesday, and Wednesday the Headmaster spoke — sometimes bringing in an "outside speaker" — a distinguished guest or alumnus. Thursday nights George Morgan frequently gave a piano recital. Friday night the Amen Corner master moved to the left-hand side of the stage and delivered his thoughts for the week, his place in the Corner being taken by his successor. Sunday nights was hymn-singing, with requests coming from the Seniors. The Headmaster always closed the Sunday service with his own selection — most often Hymn 94 — although occasionally, to the consternation of the Master in the Corner, the Headmaster would call for The School Alma Mater.

The Unsingable Alma Mater

As the Alma Mater had six verses of the most exquisitely-complex linguistic density, singing the Alma Mater was a torture akin to hanging by one's fingernails over an open flame. The catch was that one was expected *to know* the words. New boys were confronted with this task immediately on arrival at the school, and by the third or fourth week were expected to be letter-perfect. Poor souls who had difficulty memorizing the words were pilloried on the stage during Job Assembly by being forced to stumble through some semi-satisfactory version in front of all the school. The only tangible reward for this cruel and inhuman punishment was that the victim could expect to pocket a number of pennies thrown at him derisively from the audience.

In any event, nearly everyone finally managed to get down a creditable version of the first verse: ("O kind firm molder..."), but the going became increasingly harrowing as one lurched from verse to verse. By the time one was at the sixth verse (having skipped the fifth) perspiration was on his brow. As with the Lord's Prayer, some strong-minded poor memorizers were finally brave enough to defy convention and open their hymnal so that they could read the words — preferring this loss of face to the overwhelming humiliation of breaking down completely between verses three and four.

Harry Stearns graduated from Choate in 1918, where he was a roommate and classmate of Adlai E. Stevenson. After graduating from Yale in 1922, he embarked on his long career in teaching, first returning to Choate and then going on to Westminster and the John Burroughs School in St. Louis. He came to Taft in 1928, the same year he acquired an M.A. from Harvard. His academic specialty was United States History, and he served as chairman of the History Department from 1954 until his retirement in 1967. Honored as a Mailliard Teaching Fellow in 1960, he was the first recipient of the Independence Foundation Chair in 1961. An avid golfer, he coached the varsity golf team for many years and was Chairman of the Greens Committee of the Watertown Country Club. In addition to participation in the Watertown Library and the Watertown Historical Society, Harry had an interest in old railroads and was a great Red Sox fan. At his retirement after 38 years at Taft, he served until 1971 as the school's first historian and archivist. Harry and his wife Isabelle (Ibbie) had for many years a summer cottage in Waterville Valley, New Hampshire, and Harry died there August 26, 1979. At the burial service there Lance Odden aptly described Harry Stearns: "A man of great integrity, in the sense of integrating his basic beliefs with everything he did in life."

119

When Sunday Vespers was eliminated, the traditional hymn-singing feature was retained and the whole concept shifted to Wednesday evening. The other evenings of the week were also reordered: Monday and Friday evenings were available to faculty and students who wished to speak — although in practice the Headmaster continued to shoulder responsibility for these evenings. On these evenings the final hymn and the Lord's Prayer were abolished. Tuesdays and Thursdays were the province of the School Chaplain, and these services concluded with a hymn and the Lord's Prayer.

One result of these changes — welcomed with unfeigned relief by the faculty — was the abolishing of the hated post of the Amen Corner. Henceforward, only *one* body would be required on the platform — that of the speaker himself. The part played by music was also altered — from the organist playing a prelude at the opening of the service (he usually started five minutes before the service actually started) to having the speaker select the final hymn and gradually to elimination of the organ playing entirely.

It was also no longer necessary to have tenure before being expected to take your stand in Vespers. Instead, a more subtle, but equally effective method of persuasion was promulgated. At the beginning of the year, each faculty member was urged to take the stand at one time during the year, and was asked to express a preference for the Term which would be most acceptable. While not required, it was tacitly understood that advancement favored those who participated. In actual fact, whether because of the above-mentioned "surface" changes in the format of Vespers or because of a more fundamen-

tal change in societal patterns outside the school (most probably a combination of both), the new young masters seemed eager to do their share. And some fine platform speakers emerged. The new faculty enlivened the evening service in a way that would have astounded their predecessors. They played the piano, revealed semi-intimate glimpses into their own psyche, and in general, made the traditional Vespers anything but routine.

No longer were doors closed promptly at 6:00. Late-comers arrived and took their seats (to the horror of the older faculty) as late as five minutes after the bell.

Even the style of entering and leaving the Auditorium changed. In former days, boys were expected to be quiet from the Lincoln Lobby onwards — and monitors were stationed at intervals along the corridor to enforce the prohibition. And of course silence was expected once inside the auditorium. Here the playing of the organ helped to cover any minor verbal transgressions before the speaker rose to talk. (A digression should be made here to acknowledge the unsung role by a series of Taft organists from George Morgan to George Schermerhorn. Doing their best to vary the routine, these accomplished musicians played a variety of preludes and provided many of us with some most pleasant moments at the end of a hectic day.)

When the custom of playing the organ at Vespers ceased, it became virtually impossible to enforce the ritual of silence. The students entered talking and continued chattering until the speaker rose. At the end of the service, instead of a controlled, orderly exit procedure (Seniors first, but allowing time for faculty and guests to leave from the last two rows) the entire congregation arose simultaneously and emerged pell-mell. Faculty and faculty wives must perforce elbow their way into the madding crowd as best they could.

To sum up, as usual in behavioral changes such as these, there were both gains and losses. The informal atmosphere perhaps made audience participation more genuine and sincere. Perhaps the audience listened to vespers talks more attentively and applauded more sincerely. On the other hand, perhaps there was a loss of respect for the dignity of an occasion just as an "occasion" in and of itself. And some older faculty missed a tradition of politeness or courtesy that recognized the presence of elders.

Roland W. Tyler, known to boys and faculty alike as "Rollie," was for most of his years at Taft largely unsung and undervalued. A steady, thorough teacher of Lower Middle English, he never captured — or sought — the spotlight as did more dramatic colleagues. But the boys who labored through his basic English classes learned the fundamentals — and the glories — of the English language. Never again would they have doubts of what constituted a sentence error, or how to punctuate an adverbial clause. The frosting on the cake could be applied later, but the basic ingredients were in place and could be built on by Upper School practitioners. A natural offshoot of his love and respect for structure and logic in English grammar led to his great success as debating coach. Throughout his career at Taft, his debating teams were perennially successful; his last three years saw his teams win the Wil-liams College Debate Tournament each year and thus gain permanent possession of the Tournament Cup, emblematic of New England Independent School debate championship. To this day he remains Taft's most successful politician, representing Watertown (as a Republican) in the State Legislature for three terms — from 1951 to 1957. He attended the University of New Hampshire before transferring to Yale, where he graduated with honors in 1925. He later earned an M.A. from Boston University. After 36 years at Taft, he retired prematurely because of ill health, and with his wife Margaret, a champion tournament golfer, moved to Florida, where he died in 1978. One of his champion debaters, George Fayen '48, remembered him thus: "immensely fair, always putting the emphasis on courtesy under pressure, explanation as the best argument."

Coeducation

"Why can't a woman be more like a man?"

"I've grown accustomed to her face."

Henry Higgins' ambivalence reflects in many ways Taft's own movement toward coeducation — although it is fair to say that Taft was never as misogynistic as the professor. Indeed, the school had been flirting with the idea of including girls in the educational pattern for some time before the knot was finally tied in 1971.

The stage had been well set as a major part of the upheaval of the 1960s. Taft's traditional academic father-figure — Yale — had "gone coed" (an unwieldy phrase, but it seems to be the only one available) in 1969. Vassar had admitted men in 1969, Williams women in 1970, and even the traditionally masculine bastion of Dartmouth succumbed in 1972. On the secondary school level, Kent acquired a farm five miles up hill from the boys' campus and brought in girls as early as 1960; Choate and Rosemary Hall joined forces in 1971, while Hotchkiss did not follow suit until 1974.

Tri-School Coeducational Experiments

By the mid-'60s the process was well under way. In the fall of 1965 Taft participated in a tri-school experimental curriculum program with the nearby girls' schools of Westover and St. Margaret's. The announced purpose of the program was twofold: 1) "to make the most effective use of unusual physical facilities and specially trained faculty at each school; and 2) to realize the "opportunity and responsibility that independent schools have to experiment in educational methods."

The essential underpinnings of the program were that Taft with its superior science facilities would provide access to courses in the sciences; St. Margaret's would offer a course in the Philosophy of Religion; and Westover would provide an introductory course in Russian.

The program was not an unqualified success, principally because of the awkward and complicated logistical requirement of moving students from one campus to another in synchronization with differing time schedules. But like all noble experiments, it did provide important guidelines for future programs, and the very next summer Taft took another step toward coeducation by admitting girls to its summer enrichment program. The girls were on campus for classes only — no dormitory accommodations were provided. But the summer of 1967 saw even this major barrier fall; for the first time both girls and boys boarded at the school, as the Summer Enrichment Program enrolled 32 girls and 52 boys.

Harold Howe '36 receives the 1967 Alumni Citation of Merit Award from Mason Gross '29.

This step was, perhaps, one of the tangible results of a Faculty Long-Range Planning Committee that made a series of recommendations in 1966 — among them one that endorsed the idea of admitting girls. The Committee outlined the three most obvious methods of involving girls in the Taft educational scheme:

1) expanding the school's present cooperation with Westover and St. Margaret's
2) establishing Taft's own co-ordinate program (a separate girls' campus)
3) establishing full coeducaton on the present campus.

The Committee suggested a ratio of 2 girls to 3 boys and recommended a joint alumni-trustee-faculty committee to explore the subject further.

But 80 years of tradition are not undone overnight. A year later the Trustees urged only "further study" of coeducation, suggesting that "Taft can best serve this country's future leadership by remaining at approximately its present enrollment level." They did, however, recommend that the school continue its "present experimental programs."

Needless to say, such a cautious approach could hardly fail to satisfy the increasingly strident voices of the students. A fair sample would be Larry Bergreen's editorial in the *Papyrus* pointing out that "facilities for coeducation are not listed even under the 3rd priority category of expenditures for the future. Taft School will have its second rink, a student chapel, renovated dormitories, and even more boys before it has any girls."

The Spring 1971 issue of the Alumni Bulletin's cover photo which aroused so much emotion during the long-hair days of the 70s. Derric Parmenter '73 and Henry Hirsch '73.

Alumni Recommendation

In the spring of 1968 John Esty appointed a joint student-faculty committee to study coeducation further, and at the fall Class Agents Weekend a lively and far-reaching discussion ensued. At this time the Executive Committee of the Alumni Association happened to be a vigorous, articulate group clearly very much in favor of coeducation — the sooner the better — and without question their enthusiastic support was one of the major factors in keeping the issue of coeducation prominently before the Trustees.

In any event, at this juncture things began to move more rapidly. The on-campus student-faculty committee recommended that Taft begin adding its own girls as soon as possible. At about the same time, a capital-drive pamphlet written by English Instructor William Curran seemed to focus many of the concerns of the moment, stressing the "inevitability" of coeducation. As John Esty has said, "This time the response from alumni and friends seemed heavily in favor. For the first time we began to hear from alumni who were the fathers of girls!" (After nearly two decades of coeducation, it is almost comical to record that, according to a 1969 *Papyrus* poll, one of the concerns of both faculty and boys was the frightening prospect of facing girls at breakfast!)

November 21, 1969, marked a turning point in the struggle for coeducation at Taft, for it was at this meeting of the Board of Trustees in New York City that Headmaster Esty presented the case for it, and the Board recommended in effect that the school "determine the most feasible steps toward coeducation."

The Winter '69 issue of the *Alumni Bulletin* printed a series of letters from alumni, most of whom expressed strong support of coeducation, and in the fall of 1970, John Esty removed all doubt by announcing that Taft would accept girls in the fall of 1971.

The school's press release of September 1970 announced that enrollment for girls would initially be limited to about 20 day students and 50 boarding students. Already the school had about 50 inquiries from girls — one of the first being Wendy Hoblitzelle, daughter of Development Director Bill Hoblitzelle '49. In anticipation of the influx of girls, the school also hired Florence "Pecky" Gould, widow of Math Instructor George Gould, to serve as an Assistant Admissions Officer.

Joe Lakovitch

Joe Lakovitch served the school for 36 years as Athletic trainer, sometime coach of wrestling, track, and football, and as Assistant Director of Athletics. In addition to his involvement in the athletic program, for many years he was the genial, hard-working proprietor of the school bookstore, and in this capacity it is perhaps true to say that he was one faculty member who really did know every member of the student body. After the first week or two of the fall term, Joe never had to ask a student's name when he filled out the charge slip.

Finally, in September 1971, 82 girls passed through the portals as part of the largest enrollment in the school's history — 489. In June 1972, seven of these pioneers became the first Taft alumnae. In keeping with the admission of female students, five women were appointed to the faculty in 1971. And there were other significant "firsts" as women made their mark: Mary Baldrige '72 — in 1980, first alumna trustee; Elizabeth Lewis '81 — first girl head monitor; Robin Blackburn — in 1976, first woman department chairman (English).

Almost immediately, the girls made their mark. The very first year, two — Robin Shafer '73 and Martha Torrance '73 — were elcted monitors, while Faith Bushby '74 was elected Chairman of the Upper Middle Committee. The next year, Sharon Gogan '73 was Valedictorian for the Class of 1973. During the same period, Taft elected its first woman trustee: Katharine Gahagan, the mother of three Taft sons, joined the Board in 1972.

On the athletic field, too, Taft girls shortly began a distinguished career, with girls field hockey and soccer piling up enviable records in interscholastic competition.

At the end of his first year as headmaster — and Taft's second as a coeducational institution — Lance Odden reported that in 1973 Taft would have 170 girls, and that the presence of girls on campus had brought about a "radical change in the atmosphere of Taft. The reserved and somewhat cool spirit which characterized so many of the relationships in an earlier era has been replaced by new friendliness and concern which is heartening to all. In two short years girls have taught us much about openness and community spirit.... In sum, girls have helped us make Taft a place of joy as well as of learning."

1971 — The First Coeds

John Esty Retires

Amherst College President
Calvin Plimpton confers the
Degree of Doctor of Humane
Letters upon John Esty,
June 1970.

Early in his tenure, John Esty made it clear that he did not intend to serve a traditional term as Headmaster — that is, "for life." Ten years seemed to him about the right length of time. During the turbulent sixties, even ten years seemed an eternity to some headmasters and college presidents, many of whom bowed out after four or five years at the helm. John Esty was in his ninth year at Taft when he announced in October of 1971 that he would leave the following June. Restating his belief that headmasters should have "limited tenure," he also expressed his desire "to spend time exploring the role of independent schools within the nation's educational structure." This he did thoroughly in the next few years, writing a much-admired book, *Choosing a Private School* (Dodd, Mead 1974), and serving with the Rockefeller Foundation in New York City. In 1975, he became President of the National Association of Independent Schools, where he continues to serve with distinction.

As related in an earlier episode — playing the guitar at Vespers — John Esty demonstrated his departure from traditional roles. "I am 180 degrees different from Paul Cruikshank," he stated, and this was the absolute truth. His breezy, informal, personal style was the most obvious difference, but more substantial departures occurred throughout his nine years. The curriculum was thoroughly revised, vast changes were made in the social tone of the school, several additions were made to school buildings — the most important being the fine Hulbert Taft, Jr., Library. Without doubt, however, the most significant and most far-reaching change was coeducation, launched in his last year.

A new Headmaster's residence

John Esty's assumption of the headmastership was marked physically — and perhaps symbolically — by the school's purchase of the Lee House, across from the Curtis House on the corner of North Street, as the Headmaster's residence. Mr. and Mrs. Cruikshank had continued to live in Mr. Taft's quarters, physically attached to the school on the Dining Room Wing. The move surely did not mean that the Headmaster was more "detached" from school life, but it did give him — and his growing family — desirable breathing room and for the headmaster himself at least a slight perspective on the every day administration of the institution. It might also be noted that the attractive yard and garden of the new house made a particularly appropriate setting for "The Tent" on Alumni Day.

Inevitably, other changes occurred in the social pattern or relationship of the headmaster and the school. Katharine Esty, too, was different from her predecessor, Edith Cruikshank. Although always ready to take part in major social occasions, Katharine Esty was equally active in several organizations outside of Watertown. A talented, articulate woman, she also produced an interesting study of gypsies, *The Gypsies, Wanderers in Time* (Meredith Press, 1969).

The 1972 Alumni Citation of Merit was presented to John Esty on Alumni Day. As it so often does, the Citation caught the essence of the man, and is worth repeating here:

"Headmaster of Taft from 1963 to 1972, you served during a decade of tension and accelerating change. A mathematician by profession, baritone by avocation, bicyclist by inclination, you have administered our school with clarity and force and given articulate and intellectual leadership to the field of secondary education. In your own way you have demonstrated your deeply held convictions about the meaning of family, friends, and school, and with style and imagination encouraged the growth and renewal of our school community. While sheltering and preserving the best of our traditional values, you opened Taft to innovation and experiment.

"Your social consciousness, your unfailing good humor, and your sensitivity to the intricacies of human relations have enlightened and enlivened a generation of Taft boys — and eighty-eight girls. With a vision focused by reality, you have indeed endowed us and our school with an unsuspected grace."

"and eighty-eight girls"

LANCE AND PATSY ODDEN
HEADMASTER 1972 — PRESENT

Lance Odden

When John Esty announced his retirement, it did not take the Trustees long to find his successor. Mr. Esty's retirement was announced October 11, 1971; just three months later — on January 31, 1972 — Lance Odden was named Taft's fourth headmaster.

Born December 6, 1939, Lance Odden was raised in Princeton, New Jersey, where he attended schools until he entered Andover in the fall of 1954. At Andover, he won two letters in lacrosse, three in hockey, and was elected president of the student body. Graduating in 1957, he went on to Princeton, where he lettered in hockey in his sophomore and junior years, was head of the Chapel Association, and a member of Cottage Club. As a history major, he showed an early interest in the Far East, writing his senior thesis on the American experience in the China-Burma-India theater in World War II: "Reconsideration of the Stilwell Years."

After graduation in 1961, he planned to go to China as a participant in the Yale-in-China program, but an epidemic of cholera in China forced cancellation of the program for that year. Instead, he came to Watertown late in the summer, impressed Mildred Reilly, the Headmaster's secretary, and won a job as instructor in history.

Mr. Odden was a "natural" in the classroom and on the corridor, establishing immediate rapport with the students. He introduced a popular course in Far Eastern History as well as the sport of lacrosse. As Director of the Independent Studies Program, he was also responsible for overseeing many innovative approaches in this new, exploratory area of secondary education.

With his strong intellectual bent, he spent two summers and a full year at the University of Wisconsin, where he acquired his M.A. in history. His grad-

Lance Odden at his desk — in the same office used by all his predecessors.

uate thesis "U.S. Relations with China, 1929-31," dealt with American foreign policy in the early years of the Kuomintang regime.

Upon his return to Taft in 1967, he was named Chairman of the History Department and in 1969 was appointed Assistant Headmaster. A recipient of the Mailliard Award for Excellence in Teaching, he was for many years head coach of varsity hockey and varsity lacrosse.

In June 1963 Mr. Odden married Patricia Kearney, known as "Patsy". Another Princeton native, Patsy, like her husband, is a natural athlete, particularly enjoying skiing and skating. The couple have two children, John (or "Jake"), and Laurie.

Mr. Odden has been extremely active in professional education circles both in the Connecticut area and nationally, serving as Head of the Examining Committee of the National Association of Independent Schools. Among other lead-

In 1972 the first Matthew B. Preston Symposium was held at the school. Matt Preston of the class of 1969 died suddenly of a heart attack in the summer of 1971 while at Martha's Vineyard. At twenty, he was to have been a junior at Tufts. Family members and friends donated funds for an annual symposium in the arts as a living memorial by which members of the artistic community could be brought to Taft. The first symposium brought three eminent American writers to the school. Pictured here l. to r.: English Teacher Selden Edwards, William Styron, Jerzy Kosinski, Arthur Miller, and English Teacher Barclay Johnson.

ership positions, he has served as President of the Connecticut Association of Independent Schools, a member of the Board of Directors of the National Association of Independent Schools, Chairman of the Board of A Better Chance, Chairman of the Independent Schools Association of the New England Association of Schools and Colleges, and President of the New England Association of Schools and Colleges. In keeping with his long-time interest in athletics, he was responsible for creating the Founders League, an association of nine New England schools that established guidelines for athletic and admissions work.

In the summer of 1979, he fulfilled a long-postponed personal and professional dream of visiting China. He and Patsy, together with Lee Klingenstein '44 and his wife Daney, spent nearly two months visiting China, Japan, and Hong Kong.

Lance Odden has had an extraordinary impact on the Taft School. At this writing (1988) it appears that every aspect of his tenure as headmaster has been successful. In the tangible area, he has brought to completion two major building projects, the Cruikshank Athletic Center and the Arts and Humanities Building. On the more abstract side he has witnessed, and undoubtedly helped to produce, a major reversal in attitude on the part of the young people in his charge — a change, of course, taking place not only at Taft but throughout the nation. He has put together a diverse, talented, imaginative, hard-working faculty, the largest in the history of the school. A position at Taft is widely coveted by aspiring teachers. He has overseen the phenomenal expansion of Taft's fund-raising efforts, experiencing the satisfaction of seeing Taft's endowment grow from $4,513,505 in 1972 to more than $37,000,000 in 1989, and its annual giving from $229,000 to $1,404,789.

Beyond all this — perhaps as the underpinning for his success — he has the instinct, the intelligence, the "flair", the insight, to be in the forefront of many fundamental changes in the educational pattern of our day.

In his first remarks to the faculty in September 1972, he outlined his commitment to the role of the arts as a major element in the educative process: "Historically, we have emphasized success in intellectual and athletic endeavors and have tended to overlook the creative and aesthetic areas of this community. For many students art, music, dance and drama provide the opportunity for an initial involvement in an activity elected on their own. I can think of no greater avenues for tapping one's inner resources, one's creativity, or for coming to an understanding of one's self than through the creative arts. In the future we must value the arts along with academic and athletic activities as important avenues for the individual growth of our students."

From this point on, Taft was to mount an ever-increasing drive in all areas of the arts. Drama at Taft — always an important extra-curricular activity — took on even more importance. Academic credit was given for courses in acting. A series of spectacularly successful musicals such as *Cabaret, The Music Man, Godspell* was produced. Dance became a flourishing activity, attracting boys as well as girls and, together with a traditionally strong music department, contributing its share to the success of the dramatic productions. Mark Potter and Gail Wynne, in distinctly different styles and mediums, inspired class after class of art students to energize their own creative juices. The corridors at Taft began to glow with student art — batik, ceramic pieces, collage, as well as the more traditional watercolors and oils. All of this creative energy and excitement finally found, in 1986, its natural home in the magnificent Arts and Humanities Building wrought out of (ironically?) the former gymnasium.

Perhaps a more fundamental shift in the nation's educational atmosphere was noted by the Headmaster when he made his traditional opening remarks to the faculty in September 1974. While the country was still in the throes of the revolutionary excesses of the 60's and early 70's, Mr. Odden was one of the first educators to point the way out of the educational chaos of the day to a return to a more orderly environment. His talk represented a major turning point in the school's view of its mission in several fundamental areas: the restoration of standards, respect for authority, importance of critical evaluation.

While noting the progress the school has made in the last three or four years toward a more "open" and "humane" community, the headmaster expressed his alarm and concern about a trend away from liberal arts. "The recent moral bankruptcy of our society . . . underscores the need for education. . . which will expose our students to the breadth of man's knowledge and experience."

He noted "the erosion of academic standards in the face of new demands for egalitarianism" and rejected the "notion that students learn only through positive reinforcement or praise. Students must learn to discriminate between the best and the worst of their work. . . They must learn that not every piece of their own work will be satisfactory. A student may be friendly, co-operative, and sensitive to the problems of mankind and still write a poor history paper. . . What is crushing to a student's ego is not poor grades . . . but the indifference of teachers who do not appraise his work honestly."

Alumni Day 1975: Harmar Brereton '27 captured Taft's three living Headmasters in this marvelous photo.

The genus headmaster's unique
A rarified bird, so to speak;
But three at a time —
That's truly sublime)!
With spouses to make it complete.

Humble and Obedient

May 1975   Harmar & Eleanor

He called for the faculty to "sharpen standards and accept the burdens of evaluation, knowing that failure to do so distorts our students' sense of accomplishment even as it fails to prepare them for life in a highly challenging and competitive world."

Finally, he deplored the tendency in recent times "to question the prerogatives and wisdom of all authorities. If we teachers once erred in being too rigid, too dogmatic, I fear that we may now suffer from having too few deeply held convictions.... The qualities that distinguish exciting and effective teachers are still: passionate devotion to their work, willingness to make demands upon their students, conviction that learning is a serious business, and a commitment to calling forth the very best in each student."

While the more abstruse, philosophical aspects of the educational pattern were being discussed in faculty meetings, the mores of the student body affirmed in more tangible ways the truth of what their mentors were trying to formulate in educational jargon. Haircuts began to get shorter; jackets and neckties began to reappear (blue jeans were no longer allowed for class dress); a formal dance was revived in 1975; football again became a "respectable" sport.

This is not to say that there were not problems aplenty. Drugs became an ever-increasing concern. A *Papyrus* poll of the mid 70's showed that 150 of the responding students answered "Yes" to the question: "Have you ever smoked marijuana?" A majority said that they smoked a couple of times a week, and a substantial number even admitted to smoking while on a varsity sport. Vandalism, too, was a discouraging

problem: senseless destruction of school property seemed almost a routine reaction to the frustrations of adolescence. The Library began to lose so many books that a security system had to be installed to forestall students removing a book that they had not signed out. And around-the-clock security guards were now a necessity throughout the school to replace the more casual "night watchmen" of former days.

On a lighter note, the ephemeral fad of "streaking" — running naked across a stage, football field, or what-have-you — touched down at Taft in 1974 as it

The 1974 fad of "streaking", running naked across public areas, did not bypass Taft. An alert Papyrus photographer caught just one of several incidents that occurred that year.

In 1974 the Honorable Nelson
Rockefeller, grandfather of
Clare Pierson '74, spoke at her
graduation. Here, with Head-
master Odden, he leads the class
into graduation courtyard, fol-
lowed by Rev. Peter Holroyd,
School Chaplain, and Joseph
Cunningham, Director of
Admissions.

For many years Taft was one of
a select group of preparatory
schools invited to participate in
the Morehead Scholarship
awards at the University of
North Carolina. In 1975 Karen
Stevenson '75 and Carl Sangree
'75 both won the coveted award
for four-year full scholarships at
the University. After graduation
Karen went on to become a
Rhodes scholar at Oxford.

The New York Times
Metropolitan Report

L + + +
Sports Pages   B1

TUESDAY, DECEMBER 7, 1982
Copyright © 1982 The New York Times

New York, New Jersey, Connecticut

A Boarding School Changes Its Image But Keeps Its Goal

The New York Times / Rollin A. Riggs

Above, Lance Odden, headmaster of Taft School in Watertown, Conn. The football team, resting during halftime of a recent game, went undefeated this year. Below, Bill and Sue Morris, who are in charge of a dormitory, and their two sons visiting Tamara English, top, and Katherine Breer in their room.

By SAMUEL G. FREEDMAN
Special to The New York Times

WATERTOWN, Conn. — In their corduroys and flannel shirts, their running shoes and print skirts, the 523 students of the Taft School here could slip unnoticed into any suburban high school. Their rooms, adorned by India prints and pictures of rock stars and post cards from art museums, could pass for any middle-class teen-ager's bedroom.

But here the photograph of a father in one girl's room is an original print signed by Jill Krementz, the photographer. And the father is William Styron, the novelist.

Taft is a private boarding school, founded by the brother of a President and covered by the requisite ivy. It is a school that costs $8,800 a year to attend , a school that sends virtually every one of its graduates to college

and 25 percent of them to the Ivy League.

But here, like at other private boarding schools, things are changing. Taft has met the 1980's trying to balance an egalitarian impulse with an elite heritage, and the signs of transition abound.

"The school in which my daughter chose to enroll," said Peter Buttenheim, class of 1960 and the father of a Taft junior, Jennifer Buttenheim, "is not the same one to which I was sent by my father."

Not since 1969 has Taft required a coat and tie of its young men. And not since 1971 has Taft been a school for only young men. About 200 students now are young women. Twenty-three percent of the students receive scholarships or financial aid, compared with 15 percent four years ago.

"You don't have the snotty appearance

people think Taft would have," said John Wolter, a computer-science teacher who has also taught in public schools. "You couldn't tell a kid on scholarship here from a kid whose daddy could buy two of these schools."

But all that isn't to say the trappings of wealth and heritage are not in evidence. Spread across 200 hilly acres above this in-

dustrial town in central Connecticut, the Taft campus still suggests "old money." It has a golf course, a 44,000-volume library, a $1.7 million sports complex, stands of timber and a private pond. The older classroom and dormitory buildings have stone arches and carved wood panels. Taft owns some of the

Continued on Page B10

---

did in colleges and schools across the country. And another issue of the time-honored DAFT Papyrus made its appearance. The main feature story proclaimed: "When two beings constantly associate with each other, they begin to take on one another's characteristics." The article came to the conclusion that five faculty members were indeed beginning to resemble their dogs — and provided photographs to support the assertion.

An interesting view of the school as it was in the early 80's — ten years into Mr. Odden's tenure — was provided by an article in *The New York Times* of December 7, 1982. Written by Samuel G. Freedman after a week's visit in Watertown, the article presents an outsider's view of the school at a more or less typical moment during the exciting 1980's.

A Boarding School Changes Its Image Not Its Goal

Continued From Page B1

finest Colonial and Federal homes in Watertown for its faculty and staff.

The central roles of Taft — preparing its students for higher education and serving as a surrogate parent — have changed little since Horace Dutton Taft founded his school 92 years ago. If Taft is at all an anachronism, it does not show in the admissions office.

More parents than ever — 1,100 last year — applied for their children to attend Taft, even at $8,800 in a national recession. Their investment is in Taft's record: the admissions to prestigious colleges, the shaping of graduates who include Robert F. Wagner, the former Mayor of New York, and David Armstrong, the artist.

Other reasons, besides reputation, figure into the choice of Taft. Joe Lin's family had moved eight times in 15 years, and his parents wanted him to attend high school in one place. Framji Minwalla, the son of British-educated Pakistanis, came to Taft after his school in Karachi was closed for three months during anti-Western demonstrations. And 29 percent of Taft students are the relatives of alumni.

"But sadly — because anyone in education would echo this — part of our gain is the demise of the public school system," said Ferdie Wandelt, the director of admissions. "People sense Taft represents more of an opportunity."

Advantages Over Public School

Louis Kutscher would agree. He calls himself a believer in public education. He sent his three children to the respected public school system in Fairfield, Conn. He tried to help at home by banning television and setting study rules.

But two years ago, he decided to send his his daughter, Anne, a B- student in public school, to Taft.

"You can get an excellent education in public school if you're highly motivated and at the top of the class, or at the bottom and getting special help," he said. "But Anne was someone who was not going for A's all the time, and she was not being paid attention to."

At Taft, Anne has earned C's and D's and is ranked toward the bottom of her class. But she has received A's for effort, become 'accustomed to studying three hours a night and — on the strength of Taft's curriculum and name — has applied to such colleges as Bates and Skidmore.

Academic Program Unchanged

"We expected she'd probably get D's," Mr. Kutscher said. "But we expected she'd be challenged. And she has been."

The basic academic program of Taft would still seem familiar to a graduate of 30 years ago, said Lance Odden, the headmaster. Taft requires students to take four years of English, three of foreign language and mathematics and lesser amounts of art, history and science. Although there are substantial facilities and specialty courses — a history of Chinese Communism, biomedical ethics — Taft education continues to center on the teacher and the classroom.

It is a somewhat Darwinian world. The intellectually deficient and the socially disaffected, essentially, do not exist; they are not admitted. A class rarely has more than 12 students. The 74 teachers range from Mark Potter, an art teacher who bubbles with en-

thusiasm ("Look how beautiful that drawing is! No one has ever put together that exact combination before! Never!") to Robert Noyes, a shy man, but one who, when teaching French, suddenly seems capable of terrorizing a class into learning.

Taft sets a 10:30 P.M. curfew for all students and requires two-hour study halls for freshmen and sophomores. All students must perform chores each morning and participate in either interscholastic or intramural sports each afternoon. Extracurricular activities proliferate because most students engage in several, leaping from field hockey to the yearbook to the choir.

The Importance of Winning

Participation matters, but so, too, does winning. It is important that the football team finished undefeated this year, important, somehow, that the headmaster is also the best squash player on the campus. Students begin competing at 12 years old for admission to Taft; once there, they compete for grades and recognition and college admission.

It can be overwhelming at times.

Outside the office of Monie Hardwick, the college admissions counselor, hangs a comic strip drawn by a student. It shows a boy telling his parents he has a B- average. In the last frame, the father says, "Your mother and I have decided we don't love you anymore."

On a desk in a mathematics classroom, a student scribbled this verse from a song by the rock group The Clash:

You gotta cheat, cheat
No reason to be fair
Cheat, cheat
Or don't get anywhere
Cheat, cheat
If you can't win.

The known instances of cheating are few, but the pressures to win are manifold — from parents, the school and the students themselves. Miss Kutscher recalled that her parents refused to speak to her for two weeks when she did poorly.

"Pressure isn't necessarily bad," said Donald Oscarson, a Latin teacher. "It depends how a kid reacts. If it causes a psychological problem, that's bad. But I don't know if we want a painless society. I don't think it's wrong to feel the pain of running six miles, of staying up late to write a paper, of feeling homesickness."

Such pains are often salved by the extended family that is Taft, from the infant children of faculty members to the septuagenarian archivist to the unofficial pet, Mr. Oscarson's dog, Caesar. Students often share their deepest experiences — straight A's, bad grades, first love, breaking up — with classmates and teachers before their parents.

Ann Jaquith of Darien, Conn., for one, found Taft a refuge after her parents' divorce. Once her parents were separated, it fell to her to pass on communications between them.

"When I came to Taft," said the 17-year-old senior, "I was able to live my life for the first time in three years. It was a relief."

'I Never Felt So Cared For'

And when her father refused to pay her tuition — more divorce enmity — Mr. Odden promised she could continue to attend Taft. He also convinced her to talk to her father, which led to a rapprochement.

"I never felt so cared for," Miss Jaquith said.

But the insulation of Taft has its price. "My father almost flipped," one student said, "when I didn't know who Haig was." The moderate poverty in Waterbury shocks some students raised in what Mr. Odden called "a world without pain."

Taft, in turn, can shock the minority-group students who come on scholarships.

"Going to Taft's been a gift — and a challenge," said Joe Dillard, a 16-year-old junior from Minneapolis. "Challenges with work, challenges with people."

Some students, he said, told him his hair looked like a carpet. Others derided disco, the music he liked. No white student, he said, has ever invited him home for a weekend.

A Will to Succeed

"It's been rough academically," Mr. Dillard said. "Sometimes I wonder when it will ease up. But then I think of what it would be like to come all this way and then go back and have people see me as a failure. And then I realize, no matter what, I will make it."

For the affluent, too, Taft can teach ways of making it, as a scholar and a person.

Two years ago, Roberta Blackburn, an English instructor, was assigned to teach a difficult student, a championship wrestler and heir who had exasperated or intimidated other faculty members.

Miss Blackburn gave him a failing grade on on his first paper and called him to her office to explain why. For three frightfully long minutes, she recalled, he stood between her and the door, snapping a small chain against his palm. Finally, she told him, "It's not the worst thing in the world to fail." He began to sob.

Several months later, he asked Miss Blackburn to come with him to the new weight-lifting room in the athletic center. From a box he withdrew a plaque. It said: "This facility is given in honor of Roberta Blackburn, a teacher who cares."

Miss Blackburn said she was struck by the gesture. The boy had given the school something he wanted, without sacrifice, simply dipping into the family trust fund for $9,000. Yet his heart shone in the inscription.

The next fall, the boy became a counselor to freshmen. Miss Blackburn, meanwhile, began to lift weights.

The New York Times Rollin A. Riggs

Members of Taft's girls' varsity soccer team during a game. All students at the school are required to take part in a sport.

David Armstrong '65 returned to Taft in 1978 to present one of his fine water colors to the school. Art Instructor Mark Potter '48 on the right was David's "greatest influence. He gave me an appreciation for the beauty of nature."

It is easy to document the resurgence of energy and vitality that seemed to infuse the school as it emerged from the maelstrom of the 60's and early 70's. An editorial by Marsha Weinstein '78 in the October 26, '77 *Papyrus* expressed the new positive outlook. Although emphasizing the role of women (the editorial was entitled "You've Come a Long Way, Baby"), Marsha praised the overall atmosphere at Taft: "Teachers have made themselves ever more accessible, boosting the already excellent faculty-student relationship. . . . The arts program has obviously undergone the most changes in the past four years, with an increased amount of the academic day devoted to the arts, fostering greater student and faculty interest and involvement. . . Although no institution is infallible and is, at very least, perfectible, Taft has come a long way."

Further evidence of the healthy, vital school came from such disparate sources as a faculty emeritus and a present Taft student. Harry Stearns praised the *Pap* for being able to spell MAILLIARD — "a name that some boards have had trouble with", and "A Proud Taftie" wrote to praise the school spirit demonstrated in the school's journey to Lakeville, where Taft won five of the eight Saturday contests.

As the school began its 90th year, Pap editor Mark Ressler '80 found the school "gripped by a growing spirit of progress and enthusiasm. After ninety years of existence, many institutions might experience a lull in innovation, change or progress. But Taft, after ninety years, is moving in the opposite direction. Rather than lapsing into a state of stagnation, the school is forging ahead with bold new projects and smaller, yet invigorating changes."

Perhaps one of the more astounding letters to the *Papyrus* was one in February 1980 calling the school to task for not replacing the tattered American flag flying from HDT Tower. "Is there no respect for the American flag? . . . It is a disgrace that a school as prestigious as Taft would fly a flag above its campus that had been so badly torn to shreds." Even allowing for the jumbled syntax, that is a remarkable question from a 17-year-old student of that era.

ORIOCOS

John Bergen

John Bergen showed his mettle when he stepped into the tremendous gap created by the death of Bill Sullivan. Taking over the immense burden of College Admissions counselor, he turned in an outstanding performance without fanfare or pause for applause. He came to Taft in 1955 and left in 1976 to become Headmaster of the Polytechnic School in Pasadena, California. During these 21 years, he achieved a fine record as a superb English teacher, Department Chairman, and most notably Dean of the Faculty. A graduate of Exeter and Yale with an M.A. from Columbia, Bergen brought a scholar's vision and penetrating intelligence to all the jobs he held.

HYDROX

The 1977 editions of the Oriocos and the Hydrox. The Oriocos were organized in the 1920s by George Morgan and after his retirement continued for many years by French instructor John Noyes (shown here). The Hydrox emerged in 1976. The name was adopted because the girls mistook the name Oriocos for the popular cookies, the "Oreos." The girls came up with another cookie — the Hydrox!

Educational Exploration and Innovation in the '70s and '80s

Midway through the 1970s, the School embarked on a series of innovative projects that explored new areas in independent education. Although some of these projects had roots in the past, one or two were designed to adapt to changing conditions of the time, most particularly the shift from a structured, orderly environment supported by traditional social apparatus to a more free-wheeling, less-disciplined approach to life. One such program, the Independent Studies Program, already described on pages 112-114 was designed to give students a chance to create at least part of their own educational pattern.

The second of the new ventures — the "Values Program" — was a direct reaction to the displacement of organized religion and the slackening of family ties. An offshoot of the Values Program was a Volunteer Program which clearly had roots at Taft from the very early years of the school, and indeed reflects accurately the school's motto of service to others.

Alumni Day 1979 — Groundbreaking for the Cruikshank Field House. L. to R., Headmaster Odden, Board Chairman Horace Taft '43, former Trustee Heminway Merriman '30, Trustee Lee Klingenstein '44, Business Manager Charles Scott.

140

The Citation of Merit

Since the first awards on Alumni Day 1960, the Citation of Merit Committee has annually selected a distinguished Taft alumnus to receive the Alumni Citation of Merit: the School's highest honor, roughly akin to an honorary degree from a university. The award is made to that alumnus who, in his lifework, best typifies the motto of the school: "Not to be served, but to serve." Pictured at right is the group meeting in March 1982 at the Century Association, New York City.

Standing l. to r.: James Raymond '24, Kevit Cook '54, John Watling '53, Donald Buttenheim '33, Dudley Bahlman '40, Renfrew Brighton '43, Richard Davis '59, Edward Giobbe '51, John Logan '42. Seated: Richard Lovelace, Alumni Secretary; Henry Cooper '13, Phelps Platt '36.

Non Ut Sibi Ministretur Sed Ut Ministret

Although Mr. Taft's diary indicates that he had the Biblical passage in mind from the earliest days of the school, it is difficult to pin down the exact year that the school motto was first used in print. The school catalog for 1912 displays the seal essentially as it appears today. Originally translated as "Not to be ministered unto, but to minister," the translation was updated in the irreverent '60s to "Not to be served, but to serve."

The long-standing close relationship of Taft headmaster and student continues.

Purpose of the Values Program

The advent of coeducation enabled loyal Taft alumni like Trustee George Stephenson '53 to send daughter Lee '82 to Taft.

A memorable Masque and Dagger production: the 1979 presentation of *Cabaret*. Kristy Kunhardt '83 as Sally Bowles and Patrick Smith '80 as the Emcee gave outstanding performances.

One of the most disturbing aspects of the tumultuous '60s was the weakening of the traditional moral structure that supported teenagers in their difficult passage through the formative years. Although never a sectarian church school, Taft has had a school chaplain on the faculty virtually since the founding of the school, and in 1975, Chaplain Peter Holroyd and Headmaster Odden decided that the time had come for the school to take a more active role in restoring the structure formerly provided by the church and a close-knit family. At the time, Holroyd described the purpose and design of the experimental program in values: "Today, young people are having to face adult decisions early, but there is a void in the sources from which they were traditionally trained to deal with them. In an attempt to fill this void, Taft's first Values Program was conceived. The purpose was, in the Headmaster's words, '...to create a series of experiences which will help those involved understand the issues and problems they face at this particular point in their journey."

In its first year the program emphasized experience, basically a series of Outward-Bound-type problem-solving exercises involving such tasks as crossing a "raging torrent" with an inadequate board, two ropes, and team-work; fastening a telephone pole eight feet in the air between two trees and then getting each team member over it; and bringing each team over a cargo net suspended fifteen feet above the ground. Later, the groups explored moral and emotional values in a series of exercises which simulated value-laden situations such as sexuality and the use of drugs.

142

Student Reaction

Student reaction was positive: "I felt the program was worthwhile overall. I became closer to my group members as the day went on and I also noticed the discussions became easier and less tense in the afternoon. We also discussed things I felt important to everyday life but that you never really think about and discuss the value of." "I heard a lot of discouraging comments about this but they were wrong. I like this course and I think it helped me even though how it helped me is hard to say." "I liked the bomb shelter problem the most because it brought out some of my prejudices which I didn't know were there."

The Values Program has continued to be an important element in the education of Taft students, helping them — in the Headmaster's words —"to develop the kind of principles which will allow them to lead ethical lives concerned for the welfare of others."

As a corollary to the idealistic thrust of the Values Program, the School reinterpreted during the '70s and '80s one of the fundamental precepts implicit in Mr. Taft's School: service to others. With roots at least as far back as 1911, when Taft students led by John Lyman '14, Elmore McKee '14, and Harley Roberts founded a summer camp at nearby Black Rock for underprivileged youngsters from New Haven and Waterbury, volunteer programs for service outside the confines of the campus have come and gone. Again, for many years Chaplain Peter Holroyd served as the focal point for student volunteers who gave of themselves in schools, hospitals, and nursing homes throughout the Watertown area.

Mildred Reilly

Mildred Reilly retired in 1983 after 38 years as secretary to three headmasters: Cruikshank, Esty, and Odden. School legend has it that she saw something in young Lance Odden fresh out of Princeton and got him in to see Paul Cruikshank without an appointment on a particularly busy day.

Over the years, Taft has been served — in the literal sense — by a loyal and devoted service staff who have worked tirelessly behind the scenes to see that the school runs as smoothly outside the classroom as within it. In 1968, 40 members of the summer staff posed in front of the 70th Anniversary Science Center for a memorable group photograph. The two Hannings (at left) served the school almost from the start. James Hanning Sr. came to Taft in 1898 and retired in 1949. Jim, Jr. carried on the family tradition as Supervisor of Buildings until his own retirement in 1971. At the close of the 1987 school year five members of the Taft community retired after a total of nearly 160 years at the school.

Shown l. to r.: Ben Gedraitis (37 years with Taft), Betty Perrone (26 years), John McVerry (34 years), and Ray Fillion (34 years).
Not pictured — Mary Butterly (29 years).

At his death in 1985, it was discovered that Robert Harr, Dining Room porter for 37 years, had left his entire estate — nearly $100,000 — to the Taft School.

The Board of Trustees—1984

Since the first Board in 1926, Taft trustees have served the school with vision, courage, and generosity. The 1984 Board oversaw the construction of the new Arts and Humanities Wing.

1st row: Andrew K. Marckwald, Donald F. McCullough, Peter R. Fink (Chairman), Walter S. Rosenberry, Lance R. Odden, William H. Risley and William I. Miller.

2nd row: E. Philip Snyder, John R. Hurd, Dudley S. Taft, John L. Vogelstein, John W. Watling, Archbold D. vanBeuren and Richard L. Parish.

3rd row: William M. R. Mapel, Eugene V. Kelly, L. Clifford Schroeder, William A. Porteous, John J. Burns, Deirdre Johnson, and Richard M. Gregory.

4th row: Orton P. Camp, Mary T. Baldrige, Lee P. Klingenstein, Kitten Gahagan, Frank A. Kugeler, Robert Nagler and John A. Orb.

April 26, 1986, dedication of the
Arts and Humanities Wing.
L. to r.:
Architect Herbert Newman,
Trustees Lee Klingenstein '44,
Don McCullough '42,
Peter Fink '51,
Headmaster Odden,
Trustees Will Miller '74,
and Walter Rosenberry '49.

In 1985 Arthur Farwell '18 provided funds for a handsome
computer room. At the dedication of the room on Alumni
Day he engaged a micro-computer in a fiercely-contested
game of bridge, and later that evening danced up a storm at
the Old Guard Dinner. Some years earlier his brother John
'14 endowed the Farwell Fellowships, providing funds for faculty members to travel or study during the summer months.

Reiff House   Centennial Dormitory, Artist's Conception   *Cunningham House*

The Volunteer Program Today

In a 1987 *Alumni Bulletin,* William MacMullen '78 described the program as it was then operating at Taft. Using a garden as his metaphor, MacMullen relates how Program Director Mary Johnston recognized the "roots" of volunteer service in the early days of the school and now tends her garden of fifty volunteers, caring for them and "transplanting" them to the schools and hospitals around Watertown. "Because boarding schools can easily become self-sufficient, introverted communities," says Mary, "the program encourages students to learn about walks of life different than their own, to share their talents and resources, and to experience the joy and fulfillment that comes from serving others."

Calling the program "vibrant with activity," MacMullen states that the volunteers experience an "awesome widening of vision ... a growth and an awareness of their own strengths as well as of the world beyond Taft." In short, one of the school's philosophical cornerstones is still flourishing and being nourished by the current crop of "gardeners" in Watertown.

The third new program, however, had no clear precedent, although it also clearly deserves inclusion in the school's tradition of service to others. It extended Taft's role into a new area of public concern, namely, teachers and teaching methods.

Scheduled to be completed in May 1989, this new dormitory will provide housing for 40 students and two faculty. The faculty houses will be named in honor of two long-time faculty members, Joseph I. Cunningham and Alvin I. Reiff. Forming a quadrangle with the Hulbert Taft Library and McIntosh and Congdon Houses, Centennial Dormitory will house Upper Middlers and Seniors and is designed so that the quarters can be divided differently each year, adjusting to differing ratios of boys and girls.

Headmaster Odden continues to teach Chinese history. The Chinese characters on the blackboard spell out: "Go Taft — Beat Hotchkiss!"

Al Reiff and Trustee Sally Childs

Leslie D. Manning

Leslie Manning was undoubtedly one of the most colorful faculty members of the contemporary scene. Although hired as a Spanish teacher, he probably contributed more to the education of generations of Taft students outside the classroom. His apartment in "Paradise" was always full of boys, partaking of odd bits of food but also imbibing the warmth and kindliness of "the Old Beezer." He never drove anything but a convertible, and his BEEZ license plate instantly identified him on the road. An early career as a geologist exploring the Upper Amazon Basin qualified him for membership in the Explorer's Club and provided a fund of anecdotes for later use at Taft. Upon his retirement in 1974 after 23 years in the classroom, he became the School Archivist and set about bringing order to a haphazard assortment of photographs and miscellaneous memorabilia while still carrying on his unofficial duty as counselor and friend to everyone on the campus. Shortly before his death in 1985, the School recognized his contribution in this area by naming the archives the Leslie D. Manning Archives.

Alvin I. Reiff

Lance Odden called him "the perfect assistant headmaster" — and this was a position he filled for the last nine years of his life.

Al Reiff came to Taft in 1958 from the Thacher School, Ojai, California, where he had started teaching after graduating from Harvard. An immediate success as a teacher, Reiff was awarded a Mailliard Teaching Fellowship in 1964, and in 1969 spent a year on a teaching exchange at the Leys School, Cambridge, England. Upon his return, he began a rapid rise on the administrative side, becoming Head of the Science Department, Dean of the Upper Middle and Senior Classes, and Director of Studies. Odden said later that "Al Reiff [had] held virtually every administrative post at the Taft School." In 1979 he was appointed Assistant Headmaster and served in this capacity until his death in 1988. An *Alumni Bulletin* article called him "an intense, hard-working man with a wry sense of humor...a stickler for details, and a man who takes his job seriously." He seemed to be always in his office, constantly available for anyone, faculty and students, who needed him. He was most in demand as a faculty advisor. One former advisee said of him: "He strengthened me...he was second only to my father." The naming of one of the new faculty apartments in the Centennial Dormitory honors the memory of this outstanding schoolmaster.

The Taft Educational Center

From its modest beginning in 1975, the Taft Educational Center began to develop a unique summer program designed to share some of the aspects of private school education with fellow teachers in the public sector. The early programs were science-oriented, offering Taft's fine science facilities and experienced teachers as guides and counselors for teachers who were developing courses in the sciences.

The summer program had immediate appeal and was quickly extended to offer workshops and course work in a variety of areas. By 1987 the summer catalog described offerings that showed creative approaches to traditional academic disciplines such as science, math, history, English and modern languages, as well as workshops in library science and computer education. The various workshops emphasized practical applications of educational theory designed to help teachers solve the kind of problems they meet in the classroom from day to day.

Even if they aren't in the 4th generation category, individual classes continue the Taft legacy each year. Shown here are sons and daughters of the class of 1960, all in school in 1988. Front row left: John Tietjen '91, Elizabeth Applegate '88, Louisa McWherter '90, Sarah McKinnon '89, Lexie Goulard '91. Back row: Andrew Crocker '89, Tim Barton '90, Brooks Gregory '89, Donovan Smith '89, David DuPont '88.

Reprinted from a 1975 Alumni
Bulletin article written by Barclay
Johnson '53 and students in his
writing class. All of these men
retired in the 1980s.

THE NEW FRONT ROW

The Bird Man

JOHN NOYES

There he goes — up on his chair. "Dites-moi de m'asseoir," he pleads just short of tears. But we're still wondering how he made it, trying not to look surprised. So he springs to his desk. "Dites-moi!" he enunciates fiercely. "Assieds toi," one of us says, because where would a frog go next?

"Ah! Non, non, vous êtes un idiot!" And he drops to the floor. "Now, you know better than to use the informal with your favorite professor."

We have to smile. What a leap from nowhere to somewhere. He's not hurt; he can still scowl. No one has told us about Noyes the rock climber or Noyes the skier. This man's got spring steel knees.

"Do any of you colonialists have a question?" Oh, no! Oh, yes. There's a scurry for pencils and papers. Another last-minute quiz, God where's the bell? It rings, and immediately he goes into his crouch of fatigue and despair. French is like chocolate soufflé to him. The slightest taste and he's overjoyed, raring to jump us. But the bell tolls him back to Connecticut.

He dismisses the class for another day. He packs his French books against his gradebook as snugly as he moves the mulch around his roses. Then, turning off the light as he has done since World War II, he follows us down the hall.

We can't hear him now, of course, because he is disappearing, silently skating along the wall on the balls of his Sperry topsiders. With such a forward lean his head bobs freely — an easy "hello" to colleagues and kids coming his way and going by, spotting his new yellow corduroys.

Though nothing is written on his face, we know what he is thinking about: our homework in broken French, which he will have to mend with precision, then make us rewrite; and the snow in Vermont; and the harmony for another tune — all in one walk.

The question now is the *crouch*. Is he bent with exhaustion from thirty years at Taft — teaching French, even to teachers, running the modern language department, setting up ski clubs as fast as they fall, living sleuthfully in charge on Lower Mid corridors, singing in student choirs, directing the Oriocos for longer than anyone at Taft has done anything? Or is he simply re-coiling between the bells?

NEIL CURRIE '41

We mountain people don't see Currie so often as the forest people do. He's not quite the sherpa he used to be. No offense. We know he's the man who broke us out and beguiled us back to nature. And we went, well equipped with the best in ice axes, crampons, kayaks, tents. If you needed it to go further, higher, deeper, Currie managed to get it for you. But nowadays Currie likes to drop us on one side of the mountain and meet us on the other. And while we're up there, roped together in the wind, Currie and his coterie of urchins are trespassing through the branches, spying on birds.

Suddenly he stops, they say. Hands go out along the trail. Nothing moves in the breeze but Currie's feathery tuft of hair. There he is up ahead, cocked back under the barrels of his binoculars, dreaming. St. Francis?

No one wants to say, of course, that Currie likes birds better than people — at least no bird better than any one of us. He relishes that buoyant freedom in the sudden blueness of a perfect day. So naturally, even while he's talking with the ducks in the old water of the pond, Currie sees nothing but sky.

The point is, those sly, quick eyes close along his beak don't miss a trick outdoors, even in fog. Indoors, well, that's someplace else again. He kind of sleeps with his eyes open — particularly in meetings — pinching his brow to make you think he's worried about something someone is saying. Currie's just not the indoor type. Despite his great new courses in ecology, Man and Nature — the whole bag — and despite a chance to hustle every comer in croquet, an institution for Currie is still a matter of walls and spent air. In bio lab, the animals are caged; in faculty meetings the kids are boxed in this way and that. The only natural view is out the window. And that's where he lives — somewhere between the hawk and the great white owl — with a new perspective on us all.

150

Egad! The Lace

Herr Small

DICK LOVELACE

Some kids don't know the Lace, except through his way with books. The name Lovelace has become synonymous at Taft with Chaucer, Shakespeare, Shaw, Hardy, Conrad, and Frost. But not with e.e. cummings, whose poems the Lace is also willing and able to teach. Mr. Lovelace, though a staunch individualist in his own right, is hardly a rebel flower child of his time or ours. "Egad!" the Lace exclaims at any abuse of the language. He might have strangled cummings, the boy.

Nevertheless, this liberal conservative has weathered the tempest of change at Taft as graciously as any white-haired Prospero with bone-hard principles could. Despite outbursts of stubborn dissent, we like the way he is himself. In meetings he prefaces a "reactionary" comment with a courteous "Well . . . I don't know about that." Somehow we think that he has taken the new Taft as a personal challenge.

Probably those kids who get to know him best are those with whom he works in Independent Studies. They hear his generous laugh a lot and see the man behind the books. Even a fugitive scholar feels at home in his house. Mr. Lovelace has guided more students in a wider variety of independent work than any other teacher at Taft. As a would-be architect, photographer, traveler he thrives on diversity and seems to enjoy the extra work.

A stoic quality, kind of old-fashioned, emerges, too, when things get rough. "Courage!" he says with a smile to those harassed souls who fly by him in the halls. And the Lace keeps learning the truth of what he teaches. Three rough operations in three busy years have taken him out — flat out with patches on his eyes of all things. But back he bounces in stride, nodding and grinning on his way to class.

JOHN SMALL

Our Dads used to call him Captain Midnight — something about the way he used to surprise kids who were out of their rooms after lights as he unknowingly happened back from a drive in his Porsche. The Porsche, by the way, is no more. After that, the kids called him Mr. Clean — immaculate in body and soul, a powerhouse genie rising from a bottle of good German suds. But today we call him Small. That's his name, but ironically: he's huge in torso, strength and pizzazz — and great with kids, especially with those who are not so great but will be when he makes them see there's no other way.

Authoritarian power! Who needs it? Not Small. It neither flatters nor threatens him. He has made his separate peace with the world. Small's philosophy — by which he truly lives — has nothing to do with society and everything to do with faith in one's self. Needless to say, his power is awesome, compounding as he tries to deny it. He is a private man with little time for himself.

Small is most public at breakfast. You can't miss him. He enjoys his own table where he can breathe as he eats, understand sudden laughter, and be eloquent even with bombast. You can't miss him — pink with health from the sun he worships and suffers by. But just try to get a seat. His table is like a truck stop for long distance runners, wayward intellectuals, bearded alumni, and girls like me.

Small likes all kinds. The other day he dropped a warm hand on my shoulder, set his rarified eyes on mine no matter where I looked and said, frowning with a smile: "Dispense with the self-pity, okay? You can do it, okay?" Where does he get the self-control? Why doesn't *he* quit?

Whether Small gets his patience from memories of the War; or from classical music and beer; or from the weight rooms (where, with one finger the "jolly red giant" helps kids out from under those dumb black weights); or from running against the distance that separates him from all the beauty he perceives; or simply from living alone — in the company of his own mind — who can say? That's not what really *matters*, anyway.

Ten years after the first girls arrived at Taft, they were firmly ensconced in important roles throughout the school. A 1981 Alumni Bulletin article "Women at Taft" quoted the Headmaster: "Girls have participated successfully and disproportionately, in every area of Taft life." The cover of that issue is reproduced here, showing representative girl leaders in their various roles: Top: Clarissa Mack '82, sports; Middle Row: Liz Lewis '81, Head Monitor; Jill Bermingham '82, sports; Mary Pye '81, Annual Editor; Bottom Row: Cindy Thibaud '81, *Papyrus* Editor; Beth Morrison '81, Masque and Dagger.

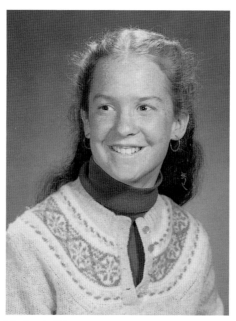

Liz Lewis '81
First Girl Headmonitor

Cooperative Ventures

The Taft Faculty—1988-1989

Under the able direction of Edward M. North, former Chairman of Taft's Science Department, the summer institute gained support from local business and foundations and shortly developed cooperative ventures with Wesleyan University and the University of Hartford to offer graduate credit to qualified participants. By 1987 the Taft Educational Center was widely recognized as an outstanding facility of its kind. In just four summers (1983-86) the Center served 1,550 teachers in 63 different workshops and issued 2,850 graduate credits through the University of Hartford. Since 1977 more than 3,300 teachers, beginning and experienced, have participated in its ever-growing numbers of programs, with an international flavor supplied by students from Spain, Venezuela, Japan, Egypt, and Israel.

Without question, the Center has been a successful bridge between the worlds of private and public education. Commenting on the success of the Center, Lance Odden pointed out that "as a center for teaching teachers and for the discussion of educational and philosophic issues, Taft is serving American society on a larger scale than ever before."

Changes In The Curriculum Through The Years

There is probably no more dramatic contrast between the Taft School of 1890 and the Taft of 1990 than the content of its curriculum. It would be useful, but impossible, to illustrate the difference photographically. The curriculum in 1890 can be readily displayed on its two brief pages. But by 1983 a full description of course offerings was published separately in a volume of 102 pages! Admittedly, these courses were to be taught during the three separate terms that then made up the academic year. Still, they amounted to 190 distinct courses, whereas in 1893 only 28 courses were offered in Taft's five-year program of that time.

The early years were, of course, heavily immersed in the classics. Both Latin and Greek were required for graduation, and all Senior classes had one recitation a week in Bible History.

Science Comes Out Of The Basement

In 1894 the curriculum was divided into two separate courses: Classical and Scientific, although the distinction was not great. Chemistry was substituted for Greek in the Middle year, and in the Senior year Physics and Botany were provided for the scientists. Nevertheless, the Scientific course designation persisted until the early 1930s. By 1932 it is no longer listed as an option. But despite meager laboratory facilities — for years the labs were in the basement under the old dining room — Science was never neglected at Taft. Sidney Hadley, Ph.D., arrived in 1922 to teach Physics and Chemistry, and he was joined in 1935 by Theophilus R. Hyde and Robert Taft Olmstead, reflecting the increased importance of Science during this period, although the physical facilities were not materially improved until the construction of the 70th Anniversary Science Center in 1961.

During the mid-'30s the catalog minced no words about the native ability of students. "Each class is divided into fast, average, and slow sections." Honors sections were available for the "more scholarly" boy so that he would not be "held back by having to remain in a class of average scholarship." He would thus be able to gain a "far more embracing knowledge of the subject."

Very early in Mr. Cruikshank's tenure, these distinctions were abandoned — at least in print. The catalog now reveals that honors sections are organized "to provide opportunity and stimulus for boys of high scholastic ability" so that they can do work which is "both in nature and amount, beyond the possibilities of those with average aptitude."

The 'Igorot' Section

And at the other end of the spectrum, the "slow" label has been dropped. Instead, boys "who have difficulty with English or a foreign language are provided with individual help and their courses are revised to provide a minimum of foreign languages." In practice, of course, the students were never fooled by labels. Upon entering the classroom and surveying their classmates, they immediately knew that they had been placed in the "igorot"* section.

Curriculum changes in languages have also reflected the changing times. As mentioned earlier, Latin and Greek were required for graduation from the start. In 1912, Greek was no longer required, although it continued to be offered as an elective until the mid 1970s. Latin persisted as a graduation requirement until the 1930s. In 1935 Latin was "ordinarily" required through the

Middle year, but was elective thereafter. Even then, under "certain circumstances," Latin could be omitted and another language substituted.

Spanish seemed to come and go in the course offerings. First appearing in 1915 as taught by Henry Morse Wells, it dropped out of sight in 1923, only to reappear in 1939. German seems to have been available from the very first year of the school and although never heavily enrolled, it endured as a modern language option. The arrival of the Kaplan Language Laboratory in 1961 greatly facilitated oral instruction in modern languages. In the mid-60s, with Russia and the U.S. straining for world leadership, Russian was added to the modern languages curriculum, and with another shift in world concerns, this time to East Asia, Chinese was offered as a language elective in 1985.

---

*"IGOROT" — Schoolboy slang for "idiot" or "ignorant."

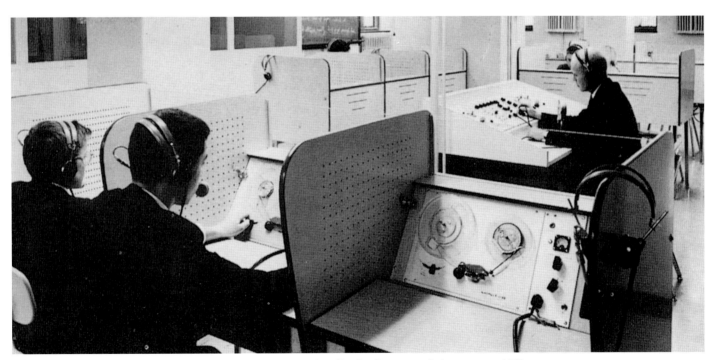

Modern Language Chairman John Noyes at the control panel — Kaplan Language Laboratory — 1961.

The curriculum changed dramatically during the nine years of John Esty's stewardship. Although never hidebound either in its academic or social structure, Taft was certainly a "traditional" school prior to 1963. Changes had, of course, been made over the years and many of the school's teaching techniques were in step with contemporary ideas.

The Drive For "Relevance"

But the curricular changes of the 1960's were more fundamental. Reflecting the philosophical upheaval of the times, the changes made student choice and student option key aspects of the new curriculum. The drive for "relevance" was another factor. No longer were students content (were they ever?) to study Latin because "it was good for you." They now wanted to know "what can it do for me?" — and not 10 or 15 years away, but "now"! A disdain for historical perspective also found a home in the new curriculum. As mentioned

earlier, such old standbys as *The Mayor of Casterbridge* were unceremoniously dumped in favor of *One Flew Over the Cuckoo's Nest*. The "New Math" sent veteran Math teachers back to summer schools to learn new approaches to an old subject. The Social Sciences were especially easy targets for student demands. Courses in Asian History, Afro-Asian Relations, Russian History, and Latin American History began to supplement or replace Medieval Civilization. By 1971, the History Department offered 25 different courses in the Upper School alone. The variety of choice available was very evident.

Perhaps the easiest target of all was anything smacking of Religion or compulsory church. Although never a "church" school, Taft has had a Chaplain virtually from the first, and for nearly 100 years some form of Bible study or Biblical History or Religion (the subject has survived various semantic disguises) has been available and generally "required." The only lapse appears to be in the turbulent '60s when Biblical History (as it was then called) was no longer required for graduation. In 1982 it reappeared as

"one unit of Philosophy and Religion" now required for graduation. Another casualty of the student upheavals was Public Speaking, which in one form or another had been a required course since 1925 in both the Upper Mid and Senior years. Its allied technique — debating — had been a pet topic of Mr. Taft's, with nearly half the school taking part in debating competitions in the early years of the school. With the retirement of Roland Tyler in 1963, Taft lost a fine debating coach and instructor in Public Speaking. The graduation requirement of Public Speaking limped along for a few years until it was dropped along with Religion in 1970.

One of the most significant curricular changes was the introduction of Advanced Placement Courses in 1958. These courses, offered in all major academic areas, provided instruction at the college Freshman level, and most major colleges granted college credit for students who passed the Advanced Placement College Board examination at the end of their Senior year at Taft. This option was a popular one, and over the years Taft compiled a proud record in the achievement of its Seniors taking the Advanced Placement exams.

Advanced Placement

The jazz band and the marching band of the 1950s are part of Taft's long musical tradition.

157

In many ways the area that demonstrates the most dramatic curricular shift is the whole field of art. In the early days the subject was rarely mentioned. Older alumni have confessed that they never felt at ease expressing an interest in sketching or painting. Rather, they endeavored to make a name for themselves in athletics, sublimating artistic pretensions for many years. Mr. Taft himself in later years came to recognize that the school had perhaps not done enough in the Arts area in the early days.

Not until 1921 does art timidly appear in the school catalog, when "Drawing and Wood Carving" are listed, and prizes offered for Drawing and Modeling. The 1923 catalog states: "When boys so desire, and when their other work permits, they are allowed to elect courses in drawing, painting, sculpture, architecture, and appreciation of pictorial art."

By 1935 art was required of Juniors and Lower Middlers one period a week; art was then an elective for the next three years of study. By 1939 the school had a full-time resident art instructor (Walter Rotan), although art was still required only at the Lower Middle level.

With the arrival of John Esty, the pace began to quicken. In his first talk to the faculty, Esty defined the role of the Headmaster: "He will know he has succeeded as a teacher of boys and as a leader of the faculty when he can see each member of the community functioning as a creative individual." The phrase "a creative individual" could well be used to highlight the emergence of art in the 1960s. The word "creative" gave its blessing to all sorts of experimentation, however crude or untutored, and in many ways seemed to suggest a departure

Dance

from the former standardized schools or disciplines. The "individual" part obviously foretold the "do your own thing" aspect of the era and again seemed to suggest absolute freedom from the strictures of the past.

Some of the strides made by the arts may be demonstrated in physical terms — in space allocation. Prior to 1960 art classes were held in the large room on the left-hand side of the corridor in Charles Phelps Taft Hall leading to Bingham Auditorium. This in itself was a step up from former quarters in H.D.T. Hall next to the Post Office —where currently the Admissions Office is located. The new Art Room had formerly been a Physics Laboratory —and before that the Lower School Study Hall. By the end of the 1960s, the Art Room had moved to the large airy room formerly used for years as the main school study hall. The room next to Bingham Auditorium was retained as an Art Room for Lower School art classes. It is a fair guess that the cubic footage allocated to art must have increased 50-fold in less than ten years.

But even more important than physical space is the quality of the "man behind the desk," and in this respect Taft has been most fortunate. Since 1955 Mark Potter '48 has been Taft's pre-eminent art instructor, developing into a gifted lecturer in Art History —one of the most popular electives in the Upper School — a first-rate water colorist in his own right, and an inspiration to developing talents such as David Armstrong '65, a nationally-known water colorist. In 1963 Sabra Johnson joined Mark Potter to initiate particularly effective art courses for Lower School students, including Taft's first explorations of ceramics. In 1970 Gail Wynne succeeded Sabra Johnson and began to develop the outstanding program now housed in the fine new Arts and Humanities Building.

For many years the school has had a policy of purchasing student art and has taken great pains to display student art in the main hallways of the school. By 1969 Senior Festival Day in the Spring Term saw more than 200 pieces of student art on display — surely evidence of "creative individualism" at the school.

Art Instructor Gail Wynne with a student at the potters' wheel.

Classics and "Combos"

For reasons lost in the mists of time, music had an earlier place than art in the school's curriculum. As early as 1912, two music instructors were listed in the catalog, one providing lessons in "Banjo, Guitar, Mandolin;" the other teaching piano and "training" the Glee Club.

But it was not until the arrival of George Morgan in 1923 that music at Taft really began to assume a significant role. Apparently even in his first year he managed to have music required for all Upper Mids: "a general listening course in the appreciation of music," and in one form or another, music was a required course from that point on. In the 1930s, music was required for Juniors and Lower Middlers, the text being "Wedge's Ear-Training and Sight-Singing." For some years music had to share the "required" label with art, until 1940 when *both* art and music were required for Lower Mids.

During the 1960s, the arts and student restlessness were inextricably intertwined. This is especially the case with music, which at that time at Taft labored through a paradoxical situation. On the one hand, it was the art form most quickly turned to by the students, caught up in the radical changes in commercial music, the Beatles, mass-produced electronic guitars, large-scale sound amplifiers. Almost anyone could play a guitar — and did. On the other hand, Taft's Music Department continued to function in the drabbest, most confining quarters of the school — the basement area under the Bingham Auditorium. But on the level immediately above the practice rooms, music was very much in evidence. Students began to give Vespers performances, playing and singing the music of the period — occasionally their own compositions.

While the vigor and vitality of the musical resurgence was undoubtedly welcomed by the Music Department, one aspect of the new interest was bothersome, namely, the tendency to perform as individuals rather than in groups. Thus, membership in the Glee Club declined, as did participation in orchestral groups such as the Concert Band. Students now preferred to play as individuals or, as the new terminology put it, in "combos." By 1972 even the school catalog recognized this trend: "Popular music groups and 'combos' are active and encouraged."

The appointment in 1963 of P.T. Young as Chairman of the Music Department smoothed the course of music during these turbulent years. Young, who had been at Taft since 1949, was a vigorous, enthusiastic teacher who had established a fine relationship with Taft students. Immediately upon taking over as Chairman, he was able to announce that Taft, for the first time, now had a full, four-year music program.

There is no question that the arts began to flourish in the ferment of the '60s. The *Papyrus* is full of art-related stores: "Famous Sculptor Exhibits at Taft;" "Vespers Talk on Modern Religious Art;" "Two Taft Pianists give Joint Recital." Headlines such as these regularly occurred week by week.

Even the stodgy catalog, probably the slowest-changing school publication, recognized the importance of the arts, when the 1967 edition listed art as a major course. Expanding and rephrasing a course description that had been virtually unchanged for twenty years, it

Music Chairman George Schermerhorn conducts the Taft Band on Mothers' Day.

now stated: "The course aims to provide the broadest possible exposure to art — to encourage a new way of seeing the world with 'the language of vision'."

And during the next decade, offerings in the arts mushroomed: by 1978, 45 elective courses in the arts were listed, and by 1980 an arts course was required for graduation: "The school recognizes the equal importance of the imaginative, emotional, aesthetic, and spiritual development encouraged by the Arts." The Arts Department now included drama and dance in addition to the old standbys of music and art, and eight or nine instructors were fully or partially engaged in the arts program.

One of the new offerings would have astounded members of the class of 1910 — Dance. The advent of girls in 1971 obviously brought about substantial changes in the entire structure of the school, perhaps nowhere so apparent as in the arts. Dance was a most appropriate medium of expression for graceful young women (although several young men also soon participated in the course), and drama was another.

The "Black Box" drama facility in the new Arts and Humanities Wing provides great flexibility for a variety of dramatic productions. In 1988 the Taft Repertory Company, directed by theater head John Sbordone, played 35 performances to schools in England, France, and throughout Connecticut. Pictured are scenes from "Godspell", "Agnes of God", and the 1988 Road Show.

For most of its existence, The Masque and Dagger had made do (and generally very well) with boys taking the parts of women, but the necessity of male selection for female roles was obviously constraining. Faculty wives often helped solve the problem, and cooperation with nearby Westover and St. Margaret's also provided welcome actresses. But as drama instructor Toby Allen '49 observed: "The general policy of permitting females to participate in major productions...widens considerably the choice of plays."

From the 1970s on, dramatic productions at Taft have gained enormously in craftsmanship, in the eyes of many, frequently reaching professional status. The phenomenal growth in interest in this aspect of education at Taft is vividly illustrated by the fact that the Theatre Arts offerings in the 1987 catalog describe ten distinct courses. To paraphrase a current cigarette advertisement: "We've come a long way!"

The Alumni Fund and Scholarship Aid

Almost from the beginning, the school has offered financial aid to families who could not afford the tuition. Certainly the spirit of the school motto was no idle boast. Mr. Taft clearly inculcated in his boys the concept that, privileged as they were, they owed something to those less privileged. Perhaps the first manifestation of this spirit was the Taft Summer Camp, founded in 1914 by a group of boys — Elmore McKee, Lane Edwards, Dunham Barney, Walter Wolf, Charles Taft and others under the guidance of Chaplain John Dallas. The first camp brought 15 youngsters from New York City to Black Rock, just outside of Watertown.

Although the first experiment was very successful, it was decided to work with boys from New Haven rather than New York for ease of transportation, and for many years the camp continued to provide both the "underprivileged" and the "privileged" with a rewarding experience.

An even earlier experience of finding scholarship boys is told in a delightful reminiscence of Neil Mallon '13:

"In the spring of 1911 Mr. Taft came to Cincinnati to visit other members of the Taft family. (The old Taft homestead is still preserved as an historic relic.) He had been at Yale with my father. So he came to dinner at our house that evening in 1911. There he met the large Mallon family of eight children, five boys and three girls. I was 16 years old and a sophomore in a public high school. The next child was my brother, John, age 15.

"Mr. Taft looked at John and me and said to my father, 'Why are not these boys at my school?' Father cast his eyes around the dinner table. He was at one end, Mother at the other end, and eight kids in between. Father said, 'Look around at this responsibility; so many to feed, and to educate; and I am just a struggling young lawyer. I can't afford the best, and the second best is quite good.'

"After dinner, Mr. Taft collared John and me in the living room and before we knew it, we were scholarship boys at Taft, as were all the other brothers when their turns came."

(from Neil Mallon's "Personal Recollections" — March 1977)

How simple and unsophisticated was scholarship selection in those days!

By the early 1920s a more formalized scheme had been set up in the form of regional scholarships. The formation of the Taft Alumni Association in 1905 had as one of its aims the idea of providing scholarship help, and by 1923 Chairman Abram Gillette '95 was able to report that the fund had in hand enough money for five scholarships and that with the hoped-for addition of one boy each from Watertown and Cleveland, they would be able to help "seven out of the ten Mr. Taft hopes to get."

Throughout the Twenties there were always one or two boys a year who were at school on what we today call "scholarships." The practice of searching out bright youngsters with thin financial backing became more and more formalized, eventually with Directors of Admission like Jack Morse and Joe Cunningham traveling to various cities each year to interview promising youngsters the local committees had discovered,

pointing them in the direction of Watertown, and subsidizing their expenses.

By 1927 the school catalog was able to announce formally: "The School gives fifteen free scholarships. Friends, chiefly alumni, of the school have given money for a few more. These are granted for high character, qualities of leadership, and intellectual ability."

A similar announcement in the 1935-36 catalog was a little more precise about qualifications: "The School has a considerable number of part scholarships available for boys of the right material in character and mind. Of course, scholarship is important, but a good all-round boy is desired, qualities of leadership being given special consideration." At this time the tuition charge was $1,450, and an "exceptional boy" might have to pay only $800 of this

"Under the Tent"

For many years each Alumni Day the tent was erected adjacent to Rockefeller Field; more recently, it has been located in the Headmaster's back yard — first on North Street, now on Guernseytown Road overlooking the golf course. Whatever the place, the tent is the Alumni Day focal point for renewing friendships with classmates and faculty.

The First Alumni Fund

charge. As Horace Taft stated in *Memories and Opinions,* "If the selection is wise, it is hard to think of an investment so rich in dividends in every way."

But the real impetus to advancing scholarship aid was coupled with the formation of the annual Alumni Fund. And this was accomplished with the arrival of Paul Cruikshank.

One of Mr. Cruikshank's first major acts was to start an annual fund drive — The Alumni Fund. Started in the fall of 1936, the 1937 Alumni Fund set a goal of $8,000; it realized just over half of that: $4,877. In succeeding years the fund did even worse, falling to $3,000 for '38 and '39 and reaching a low of $2,483 in 1942. Finally, in 1943 the fund began to climb out of the depths and gradually crept above the $5,000 level.

The most significant development came in 1950, when class solicitation was tried in a partial way. Immediately results began to prove the worth of this innovation: the 1950 fund brought in $11,000 from 29.4% of the alumni. In 1951, all solicitation was put on a class basis, with a Class Agent appointed for each class. From then on the fund never looked back.

Each year the fund bettered its previous total in dollars and number of contributors, doubling in size in the first three years. By 1960 the Fund stood at $50,000 from 52% of the alumni — a rate of participation equaled by only a handful of schools and colleges throughout the nation.

With the launching of a capital funds drive, the "Into the Sixties" drive, the school followed the conventional wisdom of the day and eliminated solicitation of the alumni fund while the capital campaign was under way. The theory of the day was that alumni could not be expected to contribute to two financial appeals in the same year. Even during the campaign itself, this theory was beginning to reveal its flaws, and by 1964 — the third and last year of the capital drive — the alumni fund began to recover. By 1965 one of the truisms of modern fund raising proved itself: Capital fund drives can *enhance* annual giving rather than frustrate it. The 1965 Fund raised $75,987, and it has increased every year since then.

Before leaving the general area of scholarship aid, it should be noted that the School always made every effort not to discriminate between scholarship students and students paying full tuition. No one except the Headmaster and the Director of Admissions knew which was which — with the exception of Regional Scholarship holders, whose status was regarded as an "honor." Scholarship students were never required to wait on tables or do extra tasks simply because they were receiving financial aid. And it is fair to say that this policy was followed by the student body as a whole: scholarship students have always been elected to key student positions and treated equally in every respect.

It was early recognized in the field of fund-raising that parents were prime givers. Indeed, most independent schools were started by wealthy parents making major capital contributions. But the idea of soliciting *all* parents on an *annual* basis did not really develop until after World War II.

The Parents' Association

At Taft, a Parents' Association had been formed to raise funds for the Field House on Rockefeller Field in 1938 and after this drive for capital funds, the Association continued to support the school each year. Their efforts were usually connected with Fathers' Day and, with suitable subtle coaching from the administration, decided upon a specific area of support that seemed realistically attainable. Most of the time, the projects were physical and aimed at immediate relief of current needs: class-room equipment, chests of drawers for bedrooms, and the like. But gradually, financial support moved to other in-tangible areas — one of the most far-sighted being the support of summer study grants for faculty members who wished to pursue advanced degrees.

By the 1950s solicitation of parents was on much the same basis as solicita-tion of the alumni: namely, the school needs — and is worthy of — your sup-port. Over the years, contributions from parents increased enormously, by the mid-1980s amounting to nearly one third of the annual funds collected.

Dramatic evidence of the growth of the Annual Fund. Alumni Day 1956: President of the Alumni Association Rutledge Bermingham '38 and Alumni Secretary Dick Lovelace present Paul Cruikshank with a facsimile check for $30,648. Alumni Day 1985: Alumni Fund Chairman Dick Gregory '60 presents Lance Odden with a similar check, this time for $1,004,892, the first million-dollar annual contribution.

Capital Funds and Buildings

Taft has never been a "wealthy" school. Although its alumni body has been very loyal in support of the Alumni Fund, large-scale gifts to endowment were few and far between. Prior to 1958, the largest single gift Taft had ever received was $500,000 from Edward Harkness in 1928. Taft's endowment per student — the most accurate measuring rod — was always substantially below that of its closest competitors for students. The school survived by running a "lean ship." Little was wasted on frills, and a hard-working faculty and staff functioned in a most efficient manner.

The financial aspects of the founding of the school and the early growth years have been covered in earlier chapters. But the generosity of Mrs. Robert Black in making the first capital investment in the school cannot be overstated and deserves reiteration. As Mr. Taft said: "I paid my debt to her financially, though there was a debt of gratitude which could never be repaid."

However, by the time the school moved to Watertown in 1893, it could, in truth, be called "Mr. Taft's School." In Watertown he undertook the next major financial step by borrowing $10,000 — to renovate the Warren House. The inclusion of Harley Roberts as one-sixth owner has also been related earlier when the school incorporated in 1912.

The first substantial capital-funds drive (as we now understand the term) was undertaken in 1927; in many ways this was the result of Mr. Taft's "clean gift" of the school to the alumni, who could now raise funds for a non-profit institution. Unfortunately, the timing was catastrophic and, again as related earlier by Mr. Taft, the stock market collapse of 1929 saw most of the pledges evaporate.

Summer study grants for faculty encourage professional growth. Pictured are 20 of the 24 teachers who received such grants in 1978.

Biff Barnard '63

Taft alumni continue to serve the school in a variety of ways after graduation. Here Bailey ("Biff") Barnard '63 chats in San Francisco with the Headmaster while serving as Chairman of the Taft Club of Northern California.

1983: Three fund raisers in a relaxed moment. Drummond Bell '63, Class Agent, Henry Estabrook '43, Chairman of the Annual Fund, and Headmaster Odden.

When Mr. Cruikshank arrived in 1936, he immediately saw the necessity for a major infusion of capital funds, for he was shocked to discover the size of the debt he had inherited. "If I had realized how much a $470,000 debt truly was I doubt that I would have ever accepted the Taft responsibility." It took Mr. Cruikshank the next twelve years to retire this "burdensome debt."

By the post-war years a series of physical additions had been undertaken principally with the support of generous individual alumni and parents. In 1948 Wade House was built as a gift of Mrs. Howard Wade in memory of her son Howard '38, who was the first Taft alumnus killed in World War II. In 1948 Rockwell Field was also developed as the primary varsity baseball diamond through the generosity of Mrs. I. H. Van Gelder.

Taft's artificial ice-hockey rink, named for Eddie Mays '27, was the first in preparatory circles — beating Andover by a few weeks. Built in 1950 largely as the result of Coach Leonard Sargent's enthusiasm and personal fund-raising, the rink has made Taft a "hockey power" for many years.

But the most major addition to the group of original collegiate gothic buildings was the addition in 1956 of a new gymnasium (never named) and the Black Squash Courts. The building cost $361,123 and provided much needed locker facilities, a basketball court, and a wrestling room, but from the very beginning it added little to the architectural elegance of the earlier mass of buildings. In a masterpiece of tactful understatement *Bulletin* Editor Robert Woolsey commented: "The building seems to fulfill the school's athletic needs without being pretentious — there is no sensation of feeling that a lot of money has been spent on frills, at the expense of basic practical needs." In 1984 the building was entirely gutted to make way for the new Arts and Humanities Center.

Another relatively minor but nevertheless important physical need of the school was adequate housing for the faculty, who were beginning to live "off campus" in increasing numbers. On Alumni Day 1958, a distinguished older alumnus, Dr. Heminway Merriman '97, was honored with the dedication of a much-needed faculty house on North Street. In 1961 five more new faculty houses were acquired. Since then, an additional 24 houses have been added.

A project of vital interest to the student body was the enlarging of the dining room, originally built in 1913, and tremendously overcrowded for many years. In 1958 Taft was able to announce that it had received a bequest of $634,000 from the estate of John B. Armstrong '34. Armstrong went from Taft to Williams and subsequently into service in World War II, when he was killed while serving as a bomber pilot. His will directed that his estate be divided equally between Taft and Williams. At the dedication a fine portrait of John Armstrong by Deane Keller '19 was unveiled — a portrait that still hangs on the south wall of the room. This physical addition enabled the school to do away with the much-

The interior of the Cruikshank Athletic Center — here set up for an Alumni Day luncheon.

The 70th
Anniversary
Development
Program

Reunions bring out the best in alumni and current students.

hated waiters' meal (held after the main meal), to get rid of the dining tables in the entrance lobby, and to replace the tables that seated fourteen (frequently with two youngsters squeezed in at the foot of the table) with more modern "boat-shaped" tables seating twelve — typically ten students and two faculty.

Another generous parent was Edward P. Snyder, father of Phil '38 and Frank '39. Much-needed fields for the rapidly growing sport of soccer were provided during the 1950s and the Snyder family later contributed Snyder Auditorium during the construction of the 70th Anniversary Science Center.

When John Esty was introduced to the school's alumni on Alumni Day, May 11, 1963, the school had just completed its most ambitious fund-raising effort — the 70th Anniversary Development Program. Chairman Ted

Luria '28 was able to announce at the Alumni Day Luncheon that more than $3,100,000 had been contributed. The largest single effort in the history of the school, the program made possible the construction of the 70th Anniversary Science Center, a 21-boy dormitory (McIntosh House), purchase or construction of 8 faculty homes, and the renovation of Horace D. Taft Building. Originally conceived as living quarters for the staff, McIntosh House has instead served (thus far) as a boys' dormitory, the School Infirmary, and (in 1984) as a girls' dormitory. One half of the total was earmarked for endowment of faculty salaries, summer study grants, scholarships, and library book funds.

At this time — June 1963 — Taft's endowment stood at $1,506,446, the annual Alumni Fund had just contributed $33,284, and the tuition for 1963-64 was $2,550. In October 1963 John Esty's arrival might perhaps have been symbolized by the razing of the Annex and the dedication of McIntosh House in the same week, "A certain poetic justice," as the *Alumni Bulletin* recorded the two occurrences. The Annex, built in 1908, had served nobly as dormitory and faculty housing. "Hundreds of boys have vivid memories of years spent within its shingled walls, and dozens of faculty families spent varying amounts of time there teaching boys, raising families, and enjoying those peculiarly close relationships that living in the Annex always seemed to encourage." *(Bulletin,* Winter 1964)

Fund-raising is hard work. For too long, Taft had "made do" with the efforts of part-time fund-raisers, people who, no matter how devoted and sincere, were basically history teachers or English teachers or whatever. When Fred Clark left to become Headmaster of the Cate School in 1964, he was replaced by Taft's first full-time fund-raiser, Clayton B. Spencer, '56, who was named Development Officer and placed in charge of all of the school's fund-raising efforts. A goal of $75,000 for the 1965 Annual Alumni Fund was set and

happily achieved a year later. In June 1965, Mr. Esty was able to say: "In the past year we have raised almost three times as much money in annual gifts as in any previous year."

In the mid-1960s the most popular indoor sport for administrators was to set up committees, and fund-raising was no exception. A Faculty Long-Range Planning Committee was organized to examine all aspects of the school. Its report, published in the Fall '66 *Alumni Bulletin,* had a number of interesting sections, among them a financial section that indicated "Capital Needs" of $12.15 million. This figure was sub-divided to include $3.5 million for facilities and $8.65 million for endowment. Foremost was an allotment of $1 million for a new library.

A comparison of endowment funds in the Fall '66 *Alumni Bulletin* clearly revealed Taft's pressing need for money in this important area:

School	Endowment
Exeter	$60 million
Andover	50 million
Groton	20 million
Loomis	10 million
Hotchkiss	8 million
Taft	3 million

The Paul and Edith Cruikshank
Athletic Center

In the fall of 1967, after reviewing the Faculty Long-Range Planning Report, the Trustees proposed a broad-based program encompassing all areas of the school's growth and involving a capital funds drive for $11 million.*

The area of highest priority for both the Faculty Long-Range Planning Report and the Trustees was the Library, and work on this important project was undertaken at once. Named in memory of Hulbert Taft, Jr. '26, the library was designed by the Hartford firm of Jeter and Cook, and was largely the gift of Mr. Taft's wife and family. The continuing interest of the Woolworth family was evidenced by the Woolworth Reference Area and the support of Norman Woolworth '45.

On December 3, 1969, the entire school helped move 25,000 books from the old Woolworth Library in the Charles Phelps Taft Building to the new Library on the other side of the pond. It is reported that the first book to enter the new library was *Ptolemy-Copernicus-Kepler,* one of the Encyclopedia Britannica's *Great Books of the Western*

World Series. It is also part of the legend of the move that an old Munich Lager Beer can was found buried away in the stacks. Students speculated that it may have been a literary aid to the Class of '07.

The fund-raising scene of the late 1960s reflected the turmoil of the times. The needs of the school were great and its physical shortcomings increasingly visible. Competition for the best students was keen, and both parents and prospective students had become increasingly sophisticated in their appraisal of a school while on an admissions tour. At the same time, outside of the school, the economy of the nation was being strained by the Vietnam War, with inflation starting its horrendous rise.

---

*A $400,000 allotment for athletic facilities mentioned new areas for basketball, squash, tennis and—amazingly—a swimming pool! The explanation . "..a recreational swimming pool was placed in second priority by the Long-Range Planning Committee, but a group of parents and alumni have made an eloquent plea for its inclusion as part of a really well rounded athletic program." The pool was never built.

Dick Parish '41 and wife Joan lead the class parade at their 40th reunion, Alumni Day, 1981. Dick's two sons are also Taft alumni, and a grandson is a member of the class of 1991.

The Kenan Challenge Grant

Business Manager Richard Pratt reported in June 1970 that the school had had a difficult year financially — ending with a deficit of $186,036. But the Capital Fund Drive was well under way. Headmaster Esty stated that the school had attained nearly $5 million (in pledges) of the $11 million goal of the campaign and in 1969 the Trustees authorized construction of a new athletic building adjoining Mays Rink. This new facility, named for James P. Logan, was actually dedicated on Alumni Day, May 13, 1972. The five new playing fields envisioned by the Trustees were also constructed at this time. The Logan Field House provided much-needed room for the popular sport of wrestling, as well as a handsome reception room, and an assortment of vital but unglamorous locker rooms, shower facilities, and offices for coaches.

At the end of the Esty era (June 1972), the Annual Fund was contributing $229,000 to the school's budget, a sharp contrast to the $33,284 raised in 1963. The school's tuition was $3,800 — a rise of 49% from the $2,550 in 1963. And the endowment had increased from $1,506,446 in 1963 to $4,526,511.

In the mid '70s Lance Odden established yet another long-range planning committee, composed as usual of a group of hard-working alumni: Dick Parish '41, Tom Chrystie '51, Henry Taft '43, plus parent Tony Wimpfheimer, and Business Manager Charley Scott. When their report appeared in 1978, the Headmaster characterized it as "a realistic and thoughtful appraisal" of the school's needs, whose intent was "to secure Taft's future as the finest independent school of its size and type in the country." The report envisioned Taft as "a middle-sized coeducational school of 500 stu-dents, primarily boarding, essentially liberal arts in curriculum, and committed to teaching character as well as mind."

The first financial goal of the report was the raising of $24,900,000, of which $5,800,000 was designated for plant development and $19,100,000 for endowment.

The first major construction project was the building of a new field house adjacent to the Logan Field House, with the underlying dual purpose of concentrating all athletic facilities on the hill and at the same time freeing the former gymnasium facilities for other use.

At the ground-breaking for the new building on Alumni Day in 1979, it was announced that the facility would be called the Cruikshank Field House, honoring Paul and Edith Cruikshank. A most imposing structure, the new field house has fulfilled its promise: the large multi-purpose portion of the building provides space for basketball, volleyball, and other indoor sports during the winter, and in the spring for indoor lacrosse, baseball, and track practice. Between this section and the Logan Field House, a two-story structure provides reception areas and four squash courts on an upper level, and ample locker space and offices on the lower level. Estimated cost of the building in 1978 was $1,300,000.

The auspicious start of the new development plan was shortly followed by the most significant event in the school's fund-raising efforts — the awarding of the Kenan Challenge Grant. In December 1980 it was announced that the William Rand Kenan Jr. Charitable Trust had awarded Taft a $2 million grant, provided that Taft raise an additional $4.5 million in endowment gifts within a three-year period.

The 70th Anniversary Science Center — built in 1961.

Headmaster Odden provided the philosophical perspective: " In the history of any great school there are periods when all possibilities are heightened and great strides can be made. The Kenan Trust has ushered us into such a period." At the same time, Director of Development Daniel Lee '67 provided the financial perspective for the challenge: "The total $6.5 million that the Kenan Challenge should generate will effectively double the size of the school's endowment."

In an unprecedented burst of financial support, over the next three years the school succeeded in meeting the Kenan Challenge — in fact raising the required challenge dollars a full six months ahead of schedule — by May 1983. In June 1983 Taft's endowment stood at $19.3 million. Encouraged by this success, the Trustees declared that meeting the Kenan Challenge was but one step on the road to achieving the goal of a $30 million endowment.

The new Arts and Humanities
Wing, skillfully integrated with
the main complex of buildings.

studio, given by the Class of 1931 on
their 55th reunion, accomodated the
growing interest that Gail Wynne had
generated in ceramics, batik, and design
in general.

While the physical part of the Long-
Range plan was being realized by the
building of the Cruikshank Athletic
Center and the Arts and Humanities
Wing, fund-raising efforts for general
operating expenses was also proceeding
apace. A series of energetic, purposeful
Annual Fund Chairmen such as Lee
Klingenstein '44, John Watling, '53,
Harry Walker '40, Henry Estabrook '43,
Dave Taylor '43, Don McCullough '42,
and Dick Gregory '60 provided the
essential man-power to stimulate successive years of astounding growth. On
Alumni Day 1987, George Utley '74,
Chairman of the Annual Fund, presented Headmaster Odden with an
outsize check for more than a million
dollars — the third such year in a row.

The seven-year period from ground-
breaking for the Cruikshank Athletic
Center on Alumni Day 1979 to the
completion of the Arts and Humanities
Wing in 1986, coupled with the growth
of the endowment from under $6 million
to $37 million between 1979 and 1989,
must surely stand as one of the most
exciting eras in its history.

As a part of the physical manifestation of the school's fund-raising success
and the completion of the plan to utilize
more effectively the former gymnasium,
the new Arts and Humanities Wing was
dedicated on April 26, 1986. The feat of
transforming the ungainly square block
of the "new" gym was magnificently
accomplished. The new wing provided
fine facilities for dance, drama, music, as
well as a much-needed student snack bar
and teachers' offices. In addition, a
beautifully-designed classroom and

Athletics

Athletics has long played a significant role in independent boarding schools. Virtually from their inception, such schools have encouraged the concept of a sound mind in a sound body. In many ways, this aspect of school life has been a distinctive difference between public and private schools. At most public schools, if a young person does not qualify for a team sport at the varsity level, he is often left with little athletic alternative except for a short period of exercise known as "gym" and consisting largely of calisthenics.

Conversely, Taft has offered each student a chance to don a uniform and to play in an organized sport at his own level of ability. For example, in the fall of 1962, there were nine different football teams. The same was true for soccer. To be sure, at the lower levels the uniforms were frequently hand-me-downs from varsity teams and the coaching was often rather amateurish. But many youngsters of indifferent athletic ability found that they could, in fact, develop athletic skills far beyond what they had earlier thought they possessed. In any event, they were out in the fresh New England air for a couple of hours and had a chance to explore a part of their growing up in a sphere distinctly different from the classroom. If a student did not shine in the classroom, perhaps the playing fields would provide another avenue of growth.

In an earlier chapter, Athletic Director Charlie Shons explored the vintage years of Taft athletics during the 1930s. Since that golden age, athletics has continued to flourish, with the advent of important additions to the school's physical plant which kept Taft teams on an equal footing with their traditional rivals. The construction of the Mays Rink in 1950, for example, without doubt contributed to the outstanding record amassed by Taft hockey teams for the next decade. During the next few years the development of the Snyder playing fields gave a much-needed boost to soccer, while in 1956 the new gym, ungainly though it may have been aesthetically, was enthusiastically received by the coaches of that day. The construction of the Logan Field House and the Cruikshank Athletic Center are reported elsewhere; in any event, by the 1980s Taft's athletic facilities were of a high order.

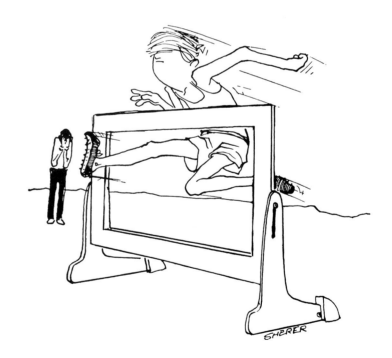

Bob Poole's High-Scoring Eleven

Although it is possible to hit only a few high spots in print, team photographs ably carry most of the historical burden of the many championship seasons. But the Bob Poole '50 football teams of the early '60s deserve mention if for no other reason than their dramatic appeal.

For two years — 1960 and 1961 — Poole's light and fast teams provided Taft football fans with a series of memorable Saturday afternoons. Week after week, Haskins Ridens '61 and Rod Moorhead '62 exploded for spectacular long runs made possible by the ball handling of quarterback Ted Carey '63 and the fake line plunges of Splinter Collins '62. In the 1960 Kent game, the team unleashed a furious attack that netted 54 points in the first half in spite of two touchdowns being called back.

The 1961 team averaged 37 points a game, losing only a heart-breaking final game to Hotchkiss.

Bob Poole stated his philosophy succinctly: "Ignore sound football principles and shoot for a touchdown on every play." For most of the season the success of this strategy so demoralized the opposition that the Taft first team could be withdrawn and the game continued with reserves. On one occasion the first team scored 38 points in the first 15 minutes and then showered and dressed at the half.

At the risk of over-emphasizing sports, it is safe to say that the impact of such a football team does a great deal to help create a school spirit that carries over into virtually every other school activity.

1961's High-scoring Eleven in action.

Football's Fall from Grace

But how quickly the times change! Just ten years later football had fallen from grace, and the Captain of the 1971 team, Peter Miller '72, had to open his review of the season with an explanation—almost an apology — for playing football in the first place:

> "At a time when a new and different emphasis is placed on individual and spiritual development, football seems outmoded. At a time when football is unpopular, the Taft varsity football participant is forced to justify the fact that he participates to others and to himself. The football player at Taft cannot compete in his violent sport blindly; he has to ask himself why."

Peter Miller goes on to do just that. He characterizes the season as having had a poor record but a "most meaningful experience. A common feeling of pride, bonds of trust and admiration, poise and sensitivity made for an experienced first string." He speaks of the team's "tenacious, courageous character" and ends on a note of pride for having captained a fine team.

The cover photograph of the Spring '71 issue of the Alumni Bulletin dramatically made his point. Undoubtedly the most explosive presentation of athletics during this period was the picture of two Taft baseball players — smiling and happy — but both with hair down to their shoulders. Inside, an article headlined "Today's Athlete: A New Breed" presented a fascinating picture of athletics at Taft at that precise moment.

The Changing Role of Athletics

The article's principal point was that most aspects of life had undergone change during the past decade and that "the role of athletics in the life of present-day students has been affected by the currents at play throughout the nation." While it was difficult to generalize, most people seemed to agree that there was more questioning of coach-centered authority and of the sacrifices involved in playing on the varsity level. "Peer prestige and self-esteem that was a part of athletics is clearly not as important today as it was ten years ago."

Whatever the extent of the disarray in 1971, the 1960s and '70s did provide yet again high points and low points, great victories and frustrating defeats, "building years" and undefeated seasons, standout natural athletes and boys who made up in determination what they lacked in natural ability.

Lacrosse

179

Football's Dramatic Come-Back

Captained by Jimmy Stone '83, son of Coach Larry Stone, the 1983 football team was undefeated in eight encounters and won the Erickson League championship.

Since coming to Taft in 1962 as Director of Athletics and head coach of football and baseball, Larry Stone has turned in an impressive record. Perhaps the most respected coach in Taft's league, he has managed to build winning teams year after year without the kind of post-graduate talent that seems to crop up in some of the opposition teams. Since 1973, Taft football teams have been champions of the Erickson League four times and co-champions twice. In baseball, too, Stone teams have turned in some fine records, most recently being champions of the Colonial League in 1984 and 1986.

Perhaps no sport better illustrates the dramatic turn-around from the low days of the early 1970s than varsity football. In 1971-72 football was condemned as a violent team sport, ill-suited to the individualistic, non-violent image then current in schools and colleges. Ten years later varsity football was dominating its competition in the Erickson League, amassing at one time an unbeaten skein of 14 straight contests. Vince Scullin '75 declared that "Coach Stone wants to win, but he wants you to have fun too. Maybe that's why Taft is about the only place where more people are playing interscholastic football than a few years ago." Rob Farrell '75 put the case: "In the '60s kids were rebelling against society's norms. Now they're more integrated, more willing to work hard for specific goals."

A relatively new arrival on the Taft athletic scene is lacrosse. First introduced by Lance Odden in 1962, lacrosse acquired varsity status in 1964 and since that time has had only one losing season!

Cross-Country's Superb Record

The record amassed by John Small's cross-country teams is astonishing. From 1959 to 1972 the team had a remarkable record of 105-17-1. Toward the end of this period they were unbeaten five seasons in a row — 54 consecutive victories. At Coach Small's retirement in 1987, the record showed 229-67-1. One of Small's talented runners, Mike Sangree '78, wrote a perceptive testimonial to Small's way with his teams in *Runner's World:* "He always creates the possibility of success."

Wrestling presents another success story. Since 1972 Coach John Wynne has compiled an impressive record with his wrestlers, for several years showing eleven wins and one defeat. In 1984-85 Taft wrestlers were Founders League champions.

Cross Country

Girls' Soccer

The Impact of Co-Education

One concern mildly expressed when Taft went coed was that the school's athletic program would suffer. Fifteen years later it is safe to say that this was one of the least-founded predictions ever made. Far from diminishing the school's athletic image, the girls have vastly enhanced it, compiling an impressive won-lost record that at times has proved a bit embarrassing to their male counterparts. During the early days, Girls Athletic Director Marion Makepeace provided the drive and enthusiasm that got the girls off to a good start.

Under Coach Rusty Davis, girls' varsity soccer achieved an outstanding record of 107-12-12 for ten of the thirteen years from 1974 to 1987. In 1988 they won the New England Championship.

The 1984 Girls Varsity Hockey Team is one of the finest the school has produced. Their final record was 20-0-1, the tie being with Groton in the Christmas Tournament. The team won the Taft-St. Paul's Girls Invitational Tournament and the Damen Eishockey Tournament in Fussen, West Germany. Coached by Patsy Odden and captained by Katey Stone '84, the team scored 133 goals while giving up only 14.

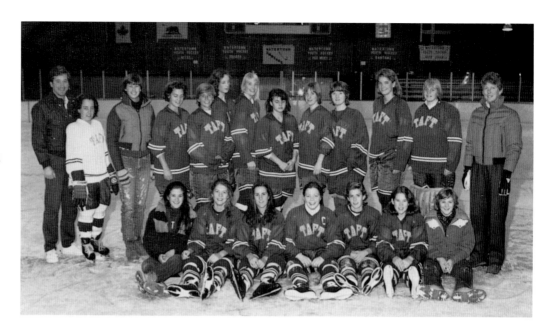

Girls' ice hockey record is perhaps even more impressive. Under Patsy Odden's skillful tutelage, girls' ice hockey has won more tournaments and produced more college players than any other Taft athletic program. For Patsy's pioneering work in girls' ice hockey, her fellow coaches (all male!) named the trophy for the New England Championship in her honor.

For some time, girls' basketball, under Coach Dick Cobb, and girls' lacrosse, under Coach Ferdie Wandelt, have also had outstanding seasons. Girls' basketball won the Western New England Championship two years in a row (1983 and 1984), while girls' lacrosse won the Founders League Championship in 1985 and was co-champion in 1987 and again in 1989.

Going Abroad

Adding a cosmopolitan flavor to athletics at Taft, varsity teams began taking their skills abroad, starting with Len Sargent's hockey team of 1968 that went to Norway, Sweden, Denmark, West Germany, Austria, and France. In 1974 girls' hockey traveled to California, in 1976 boys' soccer went to Poland, and in 1982, 1984 and 1986 girls' hockey went to Sweden and West Germany, each time winning the Damen Eishockey Turnier in Fussen, West Germany.

Perhaps the most significant difference between the modern era of athletics and that of the past is the greater variety of athletic activities available today. While past athletics tended to concentrate in a few highly-organized varsity teams, today a great many informal or intramural activities with a physical bias are offered. Today's student might well sample any of the following: weight room, road running, skiing, riding, bicycling, volleyball, dance.

Fewer Spectators — More Participants

The shift from a "spectator" to a participatory student body is most evident on football weekends, when the Headmaster is frequently asked: "Why are the stands so empty? Where are all the students?" The answer: "They're all out on the playing fields." In 1977

Athletic Director Larry Stone underscored the point: "Ten years ago Taft teams played 286 interscholastic games; this year they played 527—an increase of 85%. Obviously, you can't play and watch at the same time."

THREE YALE CAPTAINS

Derrick Niederman, John Taft, and Molly Baldridge — all members of Taft's class of 1972 — are the captains, respectively, of the squash, soccer, and women's polo teams at Yale University.

Molly Baldridge, one of Taft's first female graduates and currently a member of the Executive Committee of the Alumni Association, was the co-captain of Taft's first field hockey team.

Derrick Niederman, grandson of Orton Camp '08, is ranked among the top five college squash players in the country. At Taft, he played Varsity squash and tennis losing only one interscholastic match in three years in the latter sport.

John Taft, grandson of Robert Taft '06 (deceased) and the son of the Chairman of Taft's Board of Trustees (and Dean of Yale College) Horace Taft '43, was captain of Taft's soccer team in his senior year and an honorable mention in the All-Ivy selection last fall at Yale.

Although the Department of Sports Information at Yale keeps no records of the secondary school affiliations of Yale's team captains, a spokesman could recall no other school's having had three team captains matriculate during a single year.

Reprinted from the Spring '76
Alumni Bulletin

Taft's Second Century: Lance Odden Looks Ahead

This history opened with Horace Taft's account of the founding of the School. It is appropriate that this closing chapter be written by Taft's fourth headmaster Lance Odden. Mr. Odden sets forth here his view of the School as it is today and suggests some of the directions the School might take as it enters its second century.

If an alumnus had asked Horace Taft to make a few predictions about his School as he retired in 1936, it is unlikely that he would have anticipated much of the physical and financial reality of Taft as we approach our Centennial Year. Certainly, he would have hoped that the beliefs upon which he founded the School would endure. And so they have. From Horace Taft, we have learned the importance of simple virtues: honesty, duty, hard work and the obligation to make a difference in the lives of others in our community, in our nation and in the world. For the School's faculty, Horace Taft's most important lesson was that we should never give up on students so long as they make a determined effort, so long as they care about trying to learn. Horace Taft knew that growing up should be a challenge and that the inspiration, high standards, and wise counsel of devoted schoolmasters could make the critical difference in any young person's growth. Horace Taft also taught us that young people mature in many ways at once. Years ahead of modern psychologists, he wrote of the whole person. He knew that the journey towards learning to think for and be responsible for yourself was the essential one. He also knew this journey occurs not only in the classroom but also in the heart, spirit and actions of each student, everywhere, each day, and all in preparation for being a responsible citizen throughout life. The founder of any institution shapes the values of that community for generations to come. So it has been for The Taft School as we stand proudly by Mr. Taft's values and mission one hundred years after his courageous beginning.

If the values of Taft are remarkably unchanging, little else about the place resembles our School in its opening decade. Imagine telling Horace Taft that one day his dean of faculty would be a woman, or that nearly fifty percent of the student body would be girls, that students would come from all over the world and represent every race and creed. How proud he would be of our Summer Teaching Institute, which has educated nearly five thousand public school teachers over the past decade. Imagine what Horace Taft would have thought of the tuition, $14,300, or of the elaborate and beautiful physical plant we know today.

Many older alumni know of how skeptical he was about the value of math and science in contrast to the importance of the classics. How he would marvel and wonder about the importance of science, mathematics, computers and technology in today's curriculum. He might shudder at the thought that Chinese and Russian language stand side by side with Latin, Spanish, German and French, and he would undoubtedly wonder about the wisdom of teaching about distant continents which have so little to do with the Atlantic community so central to his time. Imagine how he would be amazed at the evolution of the facilities he constructed. The original Assembly Room first became a science lab and then the maintenance storage area. Today, the School Room, or Study Hall, is a creatively used studio for talented artists. The School's first new facility, the old gym, today houses dance, theater, photography and music. Perhaps most startling of all, modern medicine has eliminated the epidemics which were such a source of concern in Mr. Taft's day. As a result, his infirmary now is a dorm for sixty-five girls, while the Infirmary resides in a small space on the ground floor of Congdon House. However great the surprise these changes might be for our founder, I think he might marvel most at the evolution from a one building school into an integrated, collegiate-like campus with magnificent facilities surrounding the pond and up on the hill. Yet, here too, his imprint would be clear, for no school of our size and stature is more closely integrated physically or designed more carefully to insure a continuing sense of community.

If the physical changes of the last fifty years would have amazed Mr. Taft, he would also be impressed by the diversity of today's student body which represents thirty-eight states and twenty-two foreign countries and reflects the shrinking of our planet and the need to build national and international cooperation and understanding at all levels. For this diverse and talented group, Mr. Taft's belief in service remains particularly important. He would delight in our remarkable volunteer program, proudly note that monitors are still the key to community morale and leadership and that honor and trust remain the essential foundation on which the community works, even as it did in a more homogenous world with only two-hundred boys. Our School has survived and thrived because it has been a humane place, adhering to high ideals, inspiring generations of students as they learn how a community works. This same community has empowered the School's faculty and headmasters to provide leadership for the nation's secondary schools and so we have by example and by active involvement in secondary school leadership. So long as this School remains loyal to the charge that each and every individual and, indeed, our whole School, should try to make a difference in the world at large, we will continue to flourish and lead.

The 4th generation arrives! Gardner Phelps Platt, son of S. Phelps Platt III '60, grandson of S. Phelps Platt, Jr. '36, and great grandson of the late S. Phelps Platt '08, was admitted to the class of 1993 in April 1989. The Platt tradition at Taft precedes the founding of the school, for Henry B. Platt, grandfather of Phelps '36, was a classmate of Horace Taft's at Yale and entered his son at Mr. Taft's School as a result of his close friendship with Horace Taft.

185

"The Very Essence of Taft"

Inevitably, we must consider the financial underpinning of our enterprise. We should not forget that Horace Taft started his school as a "for profit" institution. He never succeeded in making a profit and when he turned over the School to the alumni, we inherited a great resource but also one with a substantial debt. While we retired that obligation decades ago, the challenge of sound financial management is unending. For over fifty years tuitions have risen dramatically, but they have not kept pace with inflation. To this day Taft has never balanced expenses with tuition income - we have never made a profit nor will we ever. However, the remarkable loyalty of alumni, parents and friends each year enables us to close the gap and balance our budget through annual giving. We are proud of our record of eighteen consecutive years of balanced budgets - a mark unmatched by any major independent school or college in the nation. This singular success leads me to dream of the day when we will have an endowment enabling us to enroll gifted students from every quarter and to do so irrespective of the need for financial aid. I also hope that our

second century will enable Taft to become an even more international school bringing together the most talented leaders from around the world. Learning to understand and respect different cultures and to work with individuals from diverse backgrounds will be essential for tomorrow's leaders who will live and work in an even smaller and more inter-dependent world. Of course, all of this assumes that alumni and parents will sustain our proud tradition of financial support as a way of building Taft for the future and of assuring that others will be able to follow in their footsteps.

In the coming decades new technologies will substantially alter the way people learn. Already, computers, language labs, interactive videos and other technology have altered the way in which we learn and teach. Always, though, there will be important lessons that come as a direct result of learning away from home, of learning to be responsible for yourself while learning to work with others who are different. Sadly, we already know that some young people are more comfortable "interacting" with technology than with

Commencement — always a popular "end of the beginning." The class of 1981 celebrates their achievement.

their fellow human beings. In our second century those essential lessons which emphasize cooperation, leadership and understanding others will be more important than ever. Learning about empathy and what it is to be a compassionate citizen must remain at the heart of our mission. Cooperation and care must stand with the drive to excel as complementary and not competing values.

I hope that our little collegiate village can become an increasingly important example of how people can work together, learn from each other and make their community a better place even as they prepare to make a difference as responsible citizens of a fragile world. I hope that Taft can increasingly demonstrate that the diverse people of the United States can live together, that we can increasingly graduate leaders committed to work for the good of others and that our School continues to serve as a benchmark of excellence in all that we undertake.

In our first century, American society passed through five major wars, through the Depression of the 1930's and the cultural upheaval of the 20's, 60's and 70's. Each generation of students and faculty was tested by unthinkable change and yet the value of going off to live with others of high purpose and principle endured. So, too, did the legacy of our founder, who believed so deeply in honor, duty, hard work, concern for others, and the ability of each of us to make a difference. "Non ut sibi ministretur, sed ut ministret." Whatever the challenges of the 21st Century, let us never forget these values, for they are the very essence of Taft. ■

Lance R. Odden, Headmaster

Some significant dates in the history of the school.

1890	Founding of the school in Pelham Manor, N.Y., as "Mr. Taft's School"; 17 boys— 3 masters; $600 boarding tuition
1893	School moves to Watertown, Connecticut, occupies Warren House; name changed to The Taft School
1894	Volume 1, #1 Papyrus (1 December)
1898	Electric lights installed
1900	First Alumni Reunion held — 30 May 78 boys — 8 masters; $600 tuition
1905	Founding of the Taft Alumni Association Oracle founded
1908	Annex built
1909	Mrs. Taft dies (December)
1910	Annex enlarged 125 boys — 12 masters; $900 tuition
1911	Gymnasium built
1912	School incorporated: Mr. Taft owns 5/6; Harley Roberts owns 1/6
1914	Horace D. Taft Building built
1915	Diplomas awarded for the first time
1920	258 boys — 21 masters; $1,300 tuition
1922	Founding of Cum Laude Rockefeller Field constructed
1923	Alumni Bulletin, Vol. 1, #1 (December)
1926	School transferred to Board of Trustees — December 4th
1927	Infirmary and Service Building constructed (now McIntosh House and Congdon House)
1930	Charles Phelps Taft Building built 323 boys — 27 masters; $1,600 tuition Alpha, Beta and Gamma Clubs fomed First Fathers' Day
1932	Lincoln Memorial bust given
1936	Horace Taft retires; Paul Cruikshank named second headmaster
1938	Parents Field House built
1940	354 boys — 33 masters; $1,450 tuition
1942	Job Program started
1943	Horace Taft dies — 28 January; age 81 years, 1 month
1948	Rockwell Field constructed
1949	Curtis House on North Street purchased First Mothers' Day

1950   Mays Rink built
        329 boys — 37 masters; $1,650 tuition

1955   Snyder Fields constructed

1956   New gymnasium and Black Squash Courts
        constructed

1957   Roof over Mays Rink constructed

1958   Merriman House (faculty) constructed on
        North Street

1959   Armstrong Dining Room constructed

1960   334 boys — 41 masters; $3,500 tuition

1961   70th Anniversary Science Center constructed
        Kaplan Language Lab built
        5 new faculty houses acquired

1963   Paul Cruikshank retires; John Esty appointed
        Taft's third headmaster
        Congdon House converted
        Two faculty duplex houses constructed on
        Hamilton Avenue

1964   Headmaster's house purchased (the Eliot Lee
        House on North Street)

1969   Five new playing fields constructed
        Hulbert Taft, Jr., Library dedicated

1970   Logan Athletic Building constructed
        432 boys — 373 boarding, 59 day — 55
        masters; $3,500 tuition

1971   Coeducation: 82 girls admitted

1972   John Esty retires; Lance Odden named Taft's
        fourth headmaster

1979   Paul and Edith Cruikshank Athletic Center
        dedicated

1980   516 students — 400 boarding, 116 day — 73
        faculty; $6,800 tuition

1985   First million dollar Alumni Fund
        Headmaster's house on Guernseytown Road
        purchased
        Paul Cruikshank dies (December)

1986   Arts and Humanities Wing dedicated

1988-   543 students — 430 boarding, 113 day — 91
1989   faculty; $13,300 tuition

1989   Centennial Dormitory opened

Adams, Martha 58, 93
Adams, Robert 58, 93
Allen, Toby '49 163
Alling, Roger '03 51
Anable, Anthony '16 .... 30, 36
Applegate, Elizabeth '88 149
Armstrong, David '65 .... 138, 159
Armstrong, James '37 94
Armstrong, John B. '34 170
Auer, Bernhard '35 86

Bacon, Seldon '27 45
Bahlman, Dudley '40 141
Bajpai, Girja (Sir) 66
Baker, Toby 93
Baldrige, Mary '72 .... 125, 145, 183
Barnard, Biff '63 169
Barney, Dunham '14 164
Barton, Tim '90 149
Bassford, William, M.D. 107
Bell, Drummond '63 169
Bergen, John 139
Bergreen, Lawrence '68 123
Bermingham, Jill '82 152
Bermingham, Rutledge '38 167
Bingham, Henry P. 25
Black, Mrs. Robert C. 4-6, 9, 12, 168
Black, Robert C. III '33 5
Blackburn, Robin 125
Blossom, Dudley (Mrs.) 25
Bourne, William, N. '13 27
Brereton, Harmar '27 133
Brighton, Renfrew '43 141
Buckingham, Mrs. John 12, 16
Burns, John, J. 145
Bushby, Faith '74 125
Buttenheim, Donald '33 .... 79, 141
Butterly, Mary 144

Camp, Orton P. '41 145
Carey, Ted '63 178
Carmody, Terrence F. 37
Carroll, Livingston '37 81
Chapin, Edwin '27 82
Chase, Colin '52 78
Chase, Irving 37
Cheli, Ralph '37 68
Childs, Sally 148
Chrystie, Adden '76 32
Chrystie, Thomas '21 32
Chrystie, Thomas Jr. '51 32
Clark, Frederick 105, 112, 172
Clark, Shirley 83
Cobb, Richard 182
Collins, Splinter '62 178
Conant, Jud '43 64
Congdon (House) 48, 87
Conrad, Barnaby '40 94
Conrad, Barnaby III '70 94
Cook, Kevit '54 141
Cooper, Henry '13 .... 116, 141
Crawford, Joan 40
Crocker, Andrew '89 149
Cruikshank, Edith 88, 90, 117, 127
Cruikshank, Paul 43, 53-96 98, 99, 122,
                    127, 143, 154, 166, 167, 169, 174
Cunningham, Betty 83, 117
Cunningham, Rev. Herbert 16, 28
Cunningham, Joseph 56, 70, 71, 82, 93,
                             117, 135, 147, 164
Curran, William 124
Currie, Marge 83
Currie, Neil '41 150
Curtis, Kingsbury 11
Curtis, William E. 21
Cushing, William L. 4

Dallas, Bishop John 31, 33, 38, 164

Davis, Richard '59 141

Davis, Rusty 181

DeVillafranca, Rick '68 111

Dodds, Harold W. 56

Dunnock, Mildred 113

DuPont, David '88 149

Dutton, Rev. Samuel 2

Douglas, Edward 79, 95, 108, 118

Douglas, Jean 79, 118

Dribben, Seymour '27 .... 74, 82

Dwight, Timothy 5

Edwards, Lane 164

Edwards, Seldon 131

Eisenhower, Dwight 77

Ellis, Doulglas '54 78

Estabrook, Henry '43 .... 61, 64, 75, 169, 176

Esty, John 56, 90, 93, 97-123, 130

Esty, Katharine 98, 99, 127

Fairman, Hugh '54 78

Farrell, Rob. '75 180

Farwell, Arthur '18 146

Farwell, Howard 73, 75, 94

Farwell, John '14 146

Fayen, George '48 121

Fenton, Daniel 69, 75, 76, 78

Fink, Peter '51 .... 145, 146

Fillion, Ray 144

Finucane, Charles '24 .... 77, 88

Franciscus, James '53 91

Freedman, Samuel G. 136

Fry, Robert '57 73

Fusonie, Albert 58, 108

Fusonie, Mrs. Albert 58

Gahagan, Katharine 125, 145

Gedraitis, Benny 144

Geldard, Richard '53 103

Gillette, Abram 1895 164

Giobbe, Edward '51 141

Gogan, Sharon '73 125

Goss, John H. 37

Goulard, Lexie '91 149

Gould, George 105, 125

Gould, Florence 125

Grant, Catherine R.N. 41, 105, 107

Gregory, Brooks '89 149

Gregory, Richard '60 .... 145, 167, 176

Gross, Charles '64 88

Gross, Mason '29 ....88, 89, 122

Hadley, Sidney 154

Hanning, James 105, 144

Hanning, James, Jr. 144

Harkness, Edward 25, 168

Harr, Robert 144

Heermance, Radcliffe 37

Heminway, Bartow '17 37

Hill, Robert '38 77

Hirsch, Henry '73 124

Hobart, Newton 38

Hoblitzelle, Wendy '74 125

Hoblitzelle, William '49 125

Holroyd, Peter 135, 142, 143

Hooker, Richard 1895 28

Howe, Arthur 44, 46

Howe, Harold '36 122

Hudson, David '65 100

Hull, Charles '62 88

Hungerford, Charles '39 114

Hurd, John R. '60 145

Hyde, Harry '52 78

Hyde, Theophilus R. '09 154

Jackson, Richard '29 45
Jamieson, Andrew '67 103
Jessup, John K. '24 61
Johnson, Barclay '53 .... 114, 131
Johnson, Deirdre 145
Johnson, James '51 83
Johnson, Sabra 159
Johnston, Mary 147
Joline, Olin Coit 15, 38-39, 48

Kaplan (Language Lab) 155
Keller, Deane '19 .... 95, 170
Kelly, Eugene V. '55 145
Kenan, William Rand Jr. 174
Kimball, Arthur R. 37
Klingenstein, Lee '44 .... 131, 140, 145-146, 176
Knowlton, Joseph Jr. '64 110
Kosinski, Jerzy 131
Kugeler, Frank A. '60 145
Kunhardt, Kristy '83 142

Ladd, Del '44 82
LaGrange, Gerald 93, 108
Larkin, Andrew '64 100
Lakovitch, Joseph 125
Learned, John '20 78
Lee, Daniel '67 175
Lehman, Orin '38 86
Lewis, Elizabeth '81 .... 125, 152
Liebert, Herman '29 45
Logan, James P. 108, 109
Logan, John '42 ....105, 141, 174
Lovelace, Peggy 83
Lovelace, Richard 83, 141, 151, 167
Lovett-Janison, Paul 105, 109
Lowry Sisters 23
Luria, Ted '28 .... 88, 171
Lyman, John '14 143

Mack, Clarissa '82 152
Mack Maynard '27 45
MacMullen, William '78 147
MacLeish, Archibald 113
Maffit, Tom 1895 29
Makepeace, Marion 181
Mailliard, James '42 80
Mailliard, Kate 80
Mailliard, J.W. Jr. '09 80
Mailliard, Lawrence '71 80
Mailliard, Ward '65 80
Mailliard, William '35 80
Mailliard, William Jr. '60 80
Mallon, Neil '13 164
Manning, Leslie D. 148
Mapel, William, M.R. 145
Marckwald, Andrew K. '30 145
Martinez, Louis '58 86
Martin, Dr. James B. 41, 107
Mayer, Tim '62 88
Mays, Eddie '27 .... 69, 169
McCarthy, Sen. Joseph 85
McCullough, Donald '42 .... 145, 146, 176
McEvoy, Dennis 66
McKee, Elmore '14 ....37, 39, 44, 143, 164
McKinnon, Sarah '89 149
McIntosh, Andrew 36, 39, 48, 62, 66
McLean, Thomas 12
McVerry, John 144
McWherter, Louisa '90 149
Mendall, Clarence 37
Merriman, Heminway 1897 ....37, 79, 170
Merriman, Heminway Jr. '30 140
Miller, Arthur 86, 131
Miller, J. Irwin '27 82
Miller, Peter '72 179
Miller, Will '74 .... 145, 146
Monohan, Otto F. 45
Moore, William '39 114
Moorhead, Rod '62 178

Morgan, George 57, 105, 106, 120. 139, 160
Morgan, Nora 57, 106
Morrison, Beth '81 152
Morse, Jack 164
Morton, Sidney 33, 38
Myers, Len '39 114

Nagler, Robert 145
Newman, Herbert 146
Niederman, Derrick '72 183
North, Edward M. 153
Noyes, John 139, 150, 155

Odden, Lance 95, 112, 125, 129-154,
                                167, 169, 174, 175
Odden, Patsy 129, 130, 131, 182
Olmstead, Robert 35, 58, 72, 154
Orb, John A. '37 145

Palmer, James '43 64
Parish, Richard '41 .... 145, 173-174
Parmenter, Derric '73 124
Pennell, Henry 78
Pennell, Marion 78
Perronne, Betty 144
Phelps, Fanny 2
Phelps, William Lyon 44
Peirson, Clare '74 135
Platt, Henry B. 185
Platt, S. Phelps '08 185
Platt, S. Phelps Jr. '36 .... 82, 141, 185
Platt, S. Phelps III '60 185
Platt, Gardner Phelps '93 185
Plimpton, Calvin 126
Poole, Joyce '74 83
Poole, Lee 83
Poole, Robert '50 178
Porteous, William A. '55 145
Potter, Mark '48 ....24, 132, 138, 159
Pratt, Richard 174
Preston, Matthew B. '69 131
Pye, Mary '81 152

Raymond, James B. '24 141
Reade, Edwin, M.D. 105, 107, 108
Reade, Edwin Jr. '39 108
Reade, Robert '43 108
Reardon, John T. 60, 92
Reiff, Alvin I. 147, 148
Reilly, Mildred 95, 130, 143
Ressler, Mark '80 138
Ridens, Haskins '61 178
Risley, William H. '35 145
Roberts, Harley 20-24, 27, 31, 33,
                                37, 45, 48, 143, 168
Robinson, Duane 73, 94
Rockefeller, Nelson 135
Rockefeller, Sterling '24 ....82, 84, 88
Rockefeller, Mrs. William 24
Rogers, James Gamble 26
Roosevelt, Theodore 29, 38
Rosenberry, Walter '49 ....145, 146
Rotan, Walter 158

Sangree, Carl '75 135
Sangree, Mike '78 181
Sargent, Leonard 69, 105, 111, 169
Sbordone, John 162
Schermerhorn, George 120, 161
Schroeder, Clifford '49 145
Scott, Charles 140, 174
Scullin, Vince '75 180
Sexton, Harlin 58, 72
Shafer, Robin '73 125
Sheldon, C. Bayard '39 114
Sherer, Steve '57 ....75, 76, 86, 104
Sherwood, Charles '02 51
Shons, Charles 50, 58, 74, 93, 177
Shons, Jeanne 58, 74
Skouras, Spyros '41 64
Small, John 151, 181
Smith, Donovan '89 149

Smith, Pat '80 142

Sneath, Mrs. E. Hershey 23

Snyder, Edward P. 171

Snyder, E. Phil '38 .... 145, 171

Snyder, Frank '39 171

Spencer, Clayton B. '56 172

Stearns, Alfred E. 44

Stearns, Harry 105, 119, 138

Stevenson, Karen '75 135

Stock, Dr. Richard '41 107

Stone, Jimmy '83 180

Stone, Katey '84 182

Stone, Lawrence H. 180, 183

Stephenson, George '53 142

Stephenson, Lee '82 142

Stott, Room 85

Styron, William 131

Sullivan, Marietta 83, 110

Sullivan, William 58, 105, 110, 139

Sweet, Robert '40 .... 82, 89, 90

Sweet, Robert Jr. '68 103

Taft, Alphonso 2

Taft, Charles P. 2, 8, 21, 25, 38

Taft, Charles P. II '13 ....39, 70, 164

Taft, Dudley '58 .... 113, 145

Taft, Henry Waters 2, 38

Taft, Henry W. '43 174

Taft, Fanny Louise 2

Taft, Horace Dutton 1-56, 66, 70, 90, 92
                    107-108, 158, 164, 166, 168, 185

Taft, Horace '43 .... 63, 140, 183

Taft, Hulbert Mrs. 113

Taft, John '72 183

Taft, Peter Rawson 2

Taft, Peter '53 70

Taft, Robert A. '06 ....63, 77, 101, 183

Taft, Robert '35 89

Taft, William Howard 2, 28, 29, 37, 38

Taft, William H. '33 77

Taft, Winifred (Mrs. Horace) 8

Tatlock, William 6

Taylor, David '43 176

Tefft, Erastus 1895 29

Thacher, Sherman 3

Thacher, Thomas Day 1899 ....37, 56

Thibaud, Cindy '81 152

Thomas, Arthur 33, 39, 73

Thomas, Lowell 60, 68, 90

Thomas, Lowell, Jr. '42 60

Thompson, Winifred (Mrs. Horace) 10

Tietjen, John Jr. '91 149

Tittman, Harold '12 77

Torrance, Martha '73 125

Torrey, Louisa 2

Tweedy, Rev. Henry Hallam 44

Tyler, Roland 42, 58, 121, 157

Utley, George '74 176

Vallee, Rudy 40

vanBeuren, Archbold D. '75 145

Van Gelder, Mrs. I.H. 169

Vogelstein, John L. '52 145

Wade, Howard '38 .... 60, 169

Wagner, Robert '29 77

Walcott, Stuart '13 31

Walker, Harry '40 176

Wandelt, Ferdie '66 182

Ward, C. Henshaw 36

Warren Robert Penn 113

Watling, John '53 ....141, 145, 176

Weinstein, Marsha '78 138

Weld, Charles B. 33, 68, 73

Weld, Garfield 31, 33, 34, 36

Wells, Henry Morse 94, 155

Welton, Paul 33, 34, 38, 48

Whyte, William H. Jr. 87

Wiggin, Frederick 1899 37

Willkie, Wendell 60

Wilson, George 33, 38, 73, 94

Wimpfheimer, Anthony 174

Winsor, Frederick 15

Wolf, Walter '14 164

Woodward, Houston '15 31

Woolsey, Robert 105, 106, 169

Woolworth, Norman '45 173

Wynne, Gail 132, 159, 176

Wynne, John 181

Young, Philip T. 105, 107, 161